Measure for Measure
as Dialectical Art

Measure for Measure
as Dialectical Art
by William B. Bache

Purdue University Studies

Lafayette, Indiana

1969

Contents

To Maryann

Introduction

I should like to begin by acknowledging an incalculable debt to what critics have said about Shakespeare, specifically to what critics have said about *Measure for Measure*. And if I feel that the complexity, the subtlety, and the art of *Measure for Measure* have not been sufficiently demonstrated by these critics, this feeling is in no way meant to be a slur on the excellence of any worthwhile commentary or in no way meant to minimize my dependence, whether direct or indirect, on that commentary. What I have attempted to say is then a kind of homage to Shakespearean criticism.

Simply, what I have tried to do is to make clear what I take to be the artistic achievement of *Measure for Measure*. In order to do this, I have of course concentrated on the meaning that emerges out of the argument conducted by the play. What follows then is an extended essay on meaning, an essay in depth, for I have taken, as my prime critical strategy, Harold Goddard's notion that a Shakespeare play must be read in depth, that the play must be perceived more deeply each time it is considered. *Measure for Measure* is magnificent. The play is in one mode, and perforce criticism must use another mode: the play as play is inviolate and inviolable.

The first thing that ought to be said about a Shakespeare play is that it is viable. The second thing is that the play was deliberately written. Since *Measure for Measure* is metaphorically alive and since it is a Gestalt or a configuration, the play cannot be simply read. We must emotionally respond; we must submit the play to our intelligence; we must try to respond creatively to the rendered thought; we must attempt to cogently and finely express the meaning as perceived. Our primary obligation is to inspect meaning. Everything we do comes down to homage to Shakespeare, and that is what we do when we pay close attention to meaning in one of his works.

But, really, any exercise in explicating a Shakespeare play becomes a matter of considerable complication. As T. S. Eliot has so eloquently indicated, the total Shakespearean achievement is implicated in any single work. Or, to speak as D. A. Traversi would, a particular play must be considered in the context of the Shakespearean sequence. The other works of Shakespeare aid and guide our understanding of a particular work. The hope, of course, is that a kind of reciprocity results. Just as the other plays enable us to understand any one play, so an analysis of one play may enable us to better understand the other plays. Perhaps the critical aim ought to be to make clear what the essential nature of a Shakespeare play is. If this is allowed to be a valid aim, the heavily dialectical nature of *Measure for Measure* expressly fits it for examination.

Fortunately, the text of *Measure for Measure* does not present a major problem. There is only the Folio text, and the cruxes are not major. A clean text keeps the main problem of *Measure for Measure* a proper problem, a problem in understanding the play's meaning. I have deliberately avoided the kind of discussion given to *Measure for Measure* by, for example, Mary Lascelles. Rather, I have tried to explain the play by means of several poetic strategies that, I think, Shakespeare used to render his thought. And although I have tried to carefully explicate *Measure for Measure,* the utility or the value of my analysis is not for me to declare but for others to decide. In that sense too, I depend on others.

William B. Bache

West Lafayette, Indiana
December 1968

I

The Ethic of Love and Duty

In *Measure for Measure* the Shakespeare ethic of love and duty operates on dark, brutal life. Each character begins with a selfish attitude toward the world and the ways of the world, and the Duke in the guise of Friar tries, and is made to try, to do what he can to preserve life so that it may become human. Escalus and the Provost and Elbow, who represent descending levels of temporal power, have good intentions but are in themselves ineffectual. The caught characters range from Angelo, who in the first scene is given full temporal power by the Duke, down to Barnardine, who is so lost that he cannot be instructed but is finally freed. The play brilliantly catches life as it actually, essentially is: devious, disordered, uncontrolled. Within the kind of realistic world rendered by the play, the characters are forced or led or allowed to enact human justice. And the chief instruments of the resultant goodness are the Duke and Isabella, the finest human beings in the play, who realize themselves most fully as they are forced or enabled or allowed to serve God, to love, and to mend. They become able, and are best able, to extend themselves beyond themselves, to enforce the Shakespeare ethic of love and duty.[1]

The essential plot problem of *Measure for Measure*, which the farcical subplot extends and magnificently ramifies, is at the heart of the Shakespearean achievement: how man is to live and how society is to be ruled. In this play this problem is specifically and significantly expressed by the Duke as a riddle: "There is scarce truth enough alive to make societies secure, but security enough to make fellowships accurst—much upon this riddle runs the wisdom of the world."[2] The Duke was

---

[1] For an excellent discussion of the ethical presuppositions of the play see Elizabeth Marie Pope, "The Renaissance Background of *Measure for Measure*," *Shakespeare Survey*, 2 (1949), 66-82.

[2] All quotations are from *Shakespeare: The Complete Works*, edited by G. B. Harrison (New York, 1952).

a poor ruler because he was too lenient, too kind, and because a loveless, "seeming" world is too much for any ruler. At first Angelo is a bad ruler because he has no feeling, no heart; later he is a worse ruler, a tyrant, because he wishes to deny the guilt that results from his aroused feelings, the guilt that causes him to put himself above his office. The Duke as Friar uses craft to counteract the growing vice of Angelo, and thus, paradoxically, erring humanity is brought to a secure, true world.

In the first scene, as he turns the city over to Angelo, the Duke says:

> Heaven doth with us as we with torches do,
> Not light them for themselves; for if our virtues
> Did not go forth of us, 'twere all alike
> As if we had them not.

In the second scene Claudio has just been arrested because Angelo, now acting as the Duke, has enforced an old law against fornication. Claudio is talking to Lucio:

> As surfeit is the father of much fast,
> So every scope by the immoderate use
> Turns to restraint. Our natures do pursue,
> Like rats that ravin down their proper bane,
> A thirsty evil, and when we drink we die.

In the fourth scene Lucio has gone, at Claudio's behest, to Isabella, Claudio's sister, as she is about to enter the cloister of Saint Clare. He speaks to her:

> As those that feed grow full—as blossoming time,
> That from the seedness the bare fallow brings
> To teeming foison—even so her plenteous womb
> Expresseth his full tilth and husbandry.

The three passages[3] are difficult and multiply meaningful and ironic: they reach out to the ends of the play. In the first place there is a simple causal relationship: because the Duke gives power to Angelo, Angelo enforces an old law, which catches Claudio; because Claudio appeals to Lucio to be his messenger to Isabella, Isabella is persuaded to go to Angelo, who is then caught by Isabella and her goodness; because of

---

[3] See the discussions of the Claudio and Lucio passages by D. A. Traversi (in *An Approach to Shakespeare* (New York, 1956), pp. 108-110) and by S. Nagarajan (in the Introduction to *Measure for Measure* in the Signet Classic Shakespeare Series (New York, 1964), pp. XXIV-XXV).

Angelo's importunity, the Duke is able to substitute Mariana, Angelo's rejected betrothed, for Isabella at an assignation. As Angelo's vice grows, the Duke's craft must be more wide-ranging and devious and, it should be added, more desperately dependent upon others.

Each of the three passages is realized in a specific context. The Duke is giving advice; Claudio is bitter at having been caught; Lucio is trying to persuade Isabella to do something that she doesn't want to do. Further, each of the three passages is seen in an enlarging context. The Duke's lines are predicated on an ethical, inclusive view of man, man as true human being. Claudio's lines give a limited view of man, man as animal. Lucio's lines give a limited, amoral view of human beings, of man as husbandman and of woman, metaphorically, as a kind of garden. Thus, in a larger sense, each of the three passages gives a different view of human nature; each presents a different view of responsibility, of the nature of the relationship of the individual to himself, to others, to society, and even to God. One of the remarkable aspects of the passages is that Lucio's seems a perversion of the others.

Now as a matter of fact, Claudio's statement and Lucio's can be seen as being imagistically and mutually compatible: one does not deny or cancel the other. Animal life depends on plant life. "As those that feed grow full" precedes "surfeit," and both food and surfeit are related to "appetite," a concept of wide sensual associations, as *Troilus and Cressida* makes clear. Claudio and Lucio express different conclusions about life for obvious reasons: Claudio is caught, and Lucio wants to engage Isabella. Both passages image life at a grange: "seedness," "fallow," "tilth," "husbandry," and "rats" are all part of grange life. The rat is simply a necessary, natural addition to Lucio's description. And Claudio's prior passage provides the rat. It is at a grange then that a rat is the enemy and needs to be poisoned, if the harvest is to be protected.

The way of life imaged in the two passages is the way of life that would be enacted at the moated grange, a setting that is suddenly introduced into *Measure for Measure* at the beginning of Act IV. Mariana, like Sebastian in *Twelfth Night,* is the character that the poetic logic of the play demands: she is the explicit means, the implicit answer. Mariana forces the equation of Angelo with Claudio: Mariana is to Angelo what Juliet is to Claudio. And Mariana is a substitute for Isabella at the assignation. Mariana makes possible the paired lovers, the couples who are presented in descending human order at the end of the play: The Duke and Isabella; Claudio and Juliet; Angelo and Mariana; Lucio and Kate Keepdown.[4] Grange life underlies the life with which the play expressly deals; it is the natural life outside the city upon which the human community inside the city depends. It is only after Mariana comes into the city that the marriages can be effected. And marriage is the symbolic sanction Shakespeare has religion pay to the human community in order to secure it.[5] After the characters have been corrected and instructed, they are brought to the city gate, and now, only at the end, can the ceremony of marriage be properly performed, and that ceremony is off stage (with Mariana and Angelo) or in the future.

In a manner of speaking, Mariana also brings Barnardine into the city with her as part of grange life. For it is instructive that Barnardine, the most irreligious person in the play, is mentioned for the first time in the second scene of Act IV. In the following scene Barnardine's angry, brutal voice is twice heard before his attendance is announced by Pompey's remarkable "He is coming, sir, he is coming. I hear his straw rustle." Imagistically, Barnardine is from the barnyard; he is the rat from the grange. And since he is several times equated with Claudio, Barnardine is what Claudio can become. And if this is true for Claudio, then it is also true for Angelo and Lucio. Barnardine is what man is when he has lost his soul.

---

[4] Though Kate Keepdown is mentioned, she never appears on stage. At any rate, the order of the couples in *Measure for Measure* is prefigured by the explicit order of the paired lovers in *As You Like It:* Orlando and Rosalind; Oliver and Celia; Silvius and Phebe; Touchstone and Audrey.

[5] "Shakespeare's comedies also begin with trouble, end in joy and are centered in love, albeit human love. The joyful *solemnitas* of marriage is an image of happiness that ends his comedies almost as invariably as death ends a tragedy." (Nevill Coghill, "Comic Form in *Measure for Measure*," *Shakespeare Survey*, 8 (1955), 18.) J. W. Lever expands the observation: "Whatever Shakespeare's religion may have been, the main body of his work from the early comedies to *The Tempest* suggests that in his view consecrated marriage signified not only the 'happy ending' to a play but the gateway to man's fulfillment of his primary function in the natural world." (J. W. Lever, Introduction to the Arden *Measure for Measure* (London, 1965), p. XCI.)

He is existential man, man as animal. Barnardine doesn't want power, like Angelo; he doesn't want to subvert society, like Lucio; he doesn't even want security, like Claudio. He simply wants to be let alone, to drink and to sleep: to him life is as meaningless as death. He has become almost inhuman, and he seems incapable of correction. He will not feel and he cannot see.

But we aren't allowed to forget that Barnardine is still, after all, a human being. And if Barnardine is imagistically part of grange life, he is only part: Mariana has her saving graces. When she is discovered at the grange, a boy is singing to her:

> Take, O, take those lips away
>   That so sweetly were forsworn,
> And those eyes, the break of day,
>   Lights that do mislead the morn.
> But my kisses bring again, bring again,
> Seals of love, but sealed in vain, sealed in vain.

In order to help make clear the complexity of the song, I quote the following from William Empson's *Seven Types of Ambiguity:*

> In that he must *take his lips away* he is already in her presence; she is actually telling him to go, and keeping command of the situation; or if he is only present in her imagination, because she cannot forget him, still the source of her fantasy satisfaction is to pretend that he is already in her presence, that she is in a position to repel him, or pretend to repel him; and her demand would be satisfied both by an expression of her resentment and by a forgetting of her desire. But he cannot be in her presence already, because he must come and *bring again* her *kisses;* and thus, when he is not present, she confesses that she wants more of them. But, again (if perhaps he *is* present, and she is sending him back to fetch the things), he must not bring her new kisses, but only her old ones back, so as to restore her to her original unkissed condition. Notice that the metaphor from *seals* does not keep up this last pretence, which seems to be her main meaning; it is no more use giving back a *seal* when it has been broken than a kiss when you wish to revoke your kisses.

The specific reference in the song is to Angelo, to his lips and his eyes, to the light in his eyes "that do mislead the morn." The song echoes the Duke's passage that has already been given: "Heaven doth with us as we with torches do, / Not light them for themselves." Angelo's eyes have led him to this evil. After Mariana agrees to take Isabella's place, the Duke ends the scene with a clear echo of Lucio's passage: "Come, let us go. / Our corn's to reap, for yet our tithe's to sow." Mr. Empson might have suggested, if he were interested in the total play, that "sealed in vain" indicates the solution to the plot problem of the play, for everyone in the play has to break his own seal of vanity or pride before any viable social order is possible. The range of vanity in men is from Angelo's complete concern for self down to Barnardine's complete unconcern for life or death. The range of pride in women is from Isabella's early but complete rejection of the world down to Kate Keepdown's complete acceptance of it.

At the end of Act III and at the beginning of Act IV, Shakespeare presents then a shorthand statement of the dialectical movement of the play. He does this by employing three different modes: first, the riddle, upon which runs much of the wisdom of the world, the riddle posed by an uninstructed, inhuman world; second, the counter to actual vice, the recognition by the Duke of the necessity of his using craft against vice, an answer explicitly stated in octosyllabic couplets; third, not just, as in the couplets, a measure against a measure, but an affirmative, positive answer that obviates the riddle by changing the world. It may be said, I think, that in order to get the answer to the riddle, the world must be given new characters, a new setting, and the harmony of song, words added to music. As the song makes clear, the seals of vanity must be broken if the world is to be human in any meaningful way.

The song is the answer, but the song has to come from outside and out of pressing human needs, and the song has to be implemented, has to be made workable, and the world must find or be luckily given the means of its salvation. After the song the Duke enters as a "man of comfort." The Duke comes in order to bring again the kisses of Angelo to Mariana, for the Duke has already provided the way for the kisses to be brought again to Mariana. Thus, further, *again* is *a gain*. The bringing of the kisses demands that desire be aroused in Angelo, that Isabella give her aid, and that the Duke be more than the Friar, at least ultimately. The song, as it is worked out and enforced, will constitute a real gain for the world, for humanity. The means of the gain are extensive and elaborate.

Angelo is the ostensible Duke. Amoral Lucio operates with vicious effectiveness under Angelo's rule, for Angelo's law is just without being merciful or understanding and can be conveniently used by one who, like Lucio, knows how to play the game. Thus, Lucio is a kind of licensed rat in the city. Like Lucifer he deals in slander, putting a bad light on goodness and virtue and a good light on vanity, in order to bring good down and in order to promote self-interest. To him fellowship is a means, and security makes his operations possible. Lucio is at Isabella's side during her first interview with Angelo because, in addition to wanting to help Claudio, he wants Isabella to undermine Angelo. The Provost, with his asides, is there as Lucio's opposite, for the Provost is concerned with others, with a higher law: he serves the true Duke.

Lucifer means *light-bringing*,[6] and the torch and light image in the Duke's passage looks toward Lucio. For it is one of the central ironies of the play that Lucio unwittingly works for good. By calling Isabella from the cloister and by bringing her back to the city, Lucio brings Isabella to realize herself, to go so far as to be willing to serve Mariana and ultimately to join the Duke in marriage. Lucio is the one who uncovers the Friar at the end, in this way symbolically making the Duke what he has always potentially been; Lucio brings the Duke dramatically back to the world.

In II, 2, during the first interview with Angelo, these lines are spoken:

> *Isab.* I would to Heaven I had your potency
> And you were Isabel! Should it then be thus?
> No, I would tell what 'twere to be a judge,
> And what a prisoner.
> *Lucio.* [*aside to Isabella*] Aye, touch him, there's the
> vein.

---

[6] Roy Battenhouse discusses the significance of many of the names (Roy Battenhouse, "*Measure for Measure* and the Christian Doctrine of the Atonement," *Publication of the Modern Language Association*, LXI (1946), 1029-59, *passim*). In a footnote to his article on comic form, Mr. Coghill remarks that Mr. Battenhouse thinks Lucio's name suggests lightness (levity) not light (Lucifer). Mr. Coghill says that Lucio is a minor fiend (Coghill, p. 24).

Lucio's observation is like that of a prospector who discovers rich ore: the relationship of judge to prisoner and what being a judge and being a prisoner mean are pregnant considerations, a rich vein, to Lucio and for us. The play always seems to work from a tension between judge and prisoner. Isabella's first sentence above firmly establishes the equation of Angelo with Isabella, for both of them are initially self-righteous. In addition, Lucio is getting at Angelo, using Isabella to get at Angelo (*I* "touch him"). Lucio is doing here what the Duke will do with Isabella and Mariana in IV, 1. There the Duke will adopt the means of Lucio, but for an entirely different purpose.

Vein in Lucio's line is picked up by *vain* in the song, as if *vanity* is to be seen in Lucio's line here, just as *vein* is to be seen in the song there. Primarily, however, the reference in "Aye, touch him, there's the vein" is, I think, to a blood vein. Angelo, we see, is moved, impassioned, feeling blood. Lucio perceives the place of touching the vein. Thus the reference seems to be to a shambles (in which case Lucio and Isabella are butchers) or to another place of bloodletting, the prison (in which case Lucio and Isabella are executioners) or to still a third place of bloodletting (in which case Lucio and Isabella are doctors, intent upon curing illness by letting blood). The place of death or the place of health has been found, and Lucio's advice to Isabella can be seen as the advice of one butcher to another, of one executioner to another, of one doctor to another. A butcher is a natural addition to grange life; an executioner is a natural addition to city life; a doctor is a natural addition to human life.

The sealed-in vain must be released, just as the sealed-in vein must be touched. The idea of blood as well as perhaps even, by a kind of witty extension, the idea of blood sports fuses with the insistence on perception. Blood and sight push us into taking *seals* and *sealed* in the song as being *seels* and *seeled*, the notion from falconry of sewing the eyes of a hawk shut. Vanity or blood seels, prevents any human sight, forestalls the possibility of meaningful perception. Angelo was blinded by self-love, and now he has been made blind by a different love, by his desire for Isabella. Angelo's love is still only vain, in a number of senses: this vain love must be controlled and constrained, or else it will be wantonly destructive, very bloody. In a sense, the sides of *Measure for Measure* are sonnet 129, lust, and sonnet 116, true love. Of specific pertinence here is the recognition that, metaphorically, Angelo must be kept hooded or seeled until it is time for him to see, that, paradoxically, Angelo has been and will be protected through his being seeled in vain.

In order to best approach the play it seems to me essential to turn quite early to G. Wilson Knight's *The Wheel of Fire:* Its moral of love is, too, the ultimate splendour of Jesus' teaching.

Measure for Measure is indeed based firmly on that teaching. The lesson of the play is that of Matthew, V. 20:

> For I say unto you, that except your righteousness shall
> exceed the righteousness of the scribes and Pharisees,
> ye shall in no case enter into the Kingdom of Heaven.

The play must be read, not as a picture of normal human affairs, but as a parable, like the parables of Jesus. The plot is, in fact, an inversion of one of those parables—that of the Unmerciful Servant (Matthew, Xviii); and the universal and level forgiveness at the end, where all alike meet pardon, is one with the forgiveness of the Parable of the Two Debtors (Luke, Vii). Much has been said about the difficulties of *Measure for Measure*. But, in truth, no play of Shakespeare shows more thoughtful care, more deliberate purpose, more consummate skill in structural techniques, and, finally, more penetrating ethical and psychological insight. None shows a more exquisitely inwoven pattern. And, if ever the thought at first seems strange, or the action unreasonable, it will be found to reflect the sublime strangeness and unreason of Jesus' teaching.

It is part of the poetic meaning of the play that in a sense Lucio becomes "the light of the world" (an overtone of the Duke's passage that the rest of the play renders) and that Angelo, the angel, must fall before he can become a man. The Duke's lines hint at the future of Lucio and Angelo; the rest of the play uses Lucio and Angelo as two developments of the lesson contained in the Sermon on the Mount, and, once they are introduced, we should not forget Claudio, who is to be saved, and Barnardine, who apparently cannot be reclaimed. The final scene takes place at the city gate, where hidden truths are revealed and accepted.

The play then works from parallels and contrasts, from parable characters, from a series of related characters, and from comparable situations. The caught men present an order in despair and an order then is reclamation: Claudio is more repentant than Angelo; Angelo is more repentant than Lucio; Lucio more than Barnardine. Each is isolated, trapped, and each is released. Claudio, Angelo, and Lucio move into another kind of control, a control signified by the marriage tie. When the Duke is added, almost a complete list results, for security is offered by and through the trapped women: Isabella, Juliet, Mariana, Kate Keepdown. They secure the men and, through the men, society. Barnardine is just released, let go. The test of every character in *Measure for Measure* is the distance he can move into human awareness, into self-knowledge. It is the test of every character in every Shakespeare play.

At the end, Isabella performs the ultimate act of human kindness and understanding, of human awareness; thinking her brother a forfeit to the law, she kneels beside Mariana before the returned Duke, who now to her *is* temporal power, and begs for Angelo's life:

> Most bounteous sir,
> Look, if it please you, on this man condemned
> As if my brother lived. I partly think
> A due sincerity governed his deeds,
> Till he did look on me. Since it is so,
> Let him not die. My brother had but justice,
> In that he did the thing for which he died.
> For Angelo,
> His act did not o'ertake his bad intent,
> And must be buried but as an intent
> That perished by the way. Thoughts are no subjects,
> Intents but merely thoughts.

"For Angelo"—that short, strange line—can go with the preceding thought: "My brother had but justice, / In that he did the thing for which he died. / For Angelo." Claudio has to be "dead" in order for Angelo to feel remorse, to be really penitent, and in order for Isabella to make her marvelous gesture: Claudio must be "dead" in order for the world to humanly live. Isabella admits the right of justice, and she is herself, at the moment, the instrument of true mercy. In the face of what Isabella believes that justice has done, she can still plead to this bounteous sir for mercy.

Intents would seem to allow us to see the word as being *intense,* and this makes Isabella's argument extreme. It doesn't make any difference how intense the thoughts are: so long as they remain simply thoughts, they should not be punished as if they were accomplished acts. Further, Angelo wanted Claudio dead because Angelo intended to protect only himself. Angelo intended to destroy Claudio, but the Duke used craft in time in order to control Angelo's intent. Thoughts are worked out as deeds in time. Action has been submitted to time, and the audience has watched the Duke working in time, using time, finally controlling time, providing the world this particular occasion in time. A time consideration has demanded that the Duke enlist the services of the Provost, Isabella, and Mariana. We are meant to understand the pertinence of time to justice and mercy, the ultimate tension of *Measure for Measure*. At the very end when the Duke accepts his authority, he is then submitting the now-secure world to time—to time where man both comes to maturity and is destroyed, as sonnet 60 makes clear.

Exceedingly relevant to *Measure for Measure* is E. M. W. Tillyard's notion that the full pattern in a Shakespeare play presents three stages—prosperity, destruction, re-creation.[7] For in *Measure for Measure* an initial "sophisticated" world is presented; that world is destroyed, and out of that destruction emerges a real world, a truly human world. The society at the beginning of *Measure for Measure* is one of false prosperity, of "seeming"; it is divorced from actual life. And the movement of the action is in the direction of making the world more consonant with true life, with human reality. The characters are corrected and instructed. The movement is toward reality and into truth. The characters move into the light and to the city gate: roles become proper at the very end.

It may be argued, I believe, that the symbolic movement of every Shakespeare play is a movement back to an ordered world, to a garden, to a Garden of Eden existence, to a purified state. *Then* re-creation must submit itself to prosperity. For in a garden, life is idealized, what life only ideally is. Paradoxically, human life must leave the green world, the garden. Paradise must be lost if Heaven is to be won. At the end of *As You Like It*, for example, the secure world will

---

[7] See E. M. W. Tillyard, *Shakespeare's Last Plays* (London, 1951), particularly "The Tragic Pattern," pp. 16-58, *passim*.

leave the Forest of Arden and will return to the envious court. At the end of *The Tempest* secure society will go back to Naples and Milan: the lessons learned on the magic isle must be submitted to the uncontrolled and uncontrollable real world.

Clearly, *Measure for Measure* is about human action and human beings, about honor and dishonor, about freedom and responsibility, about being and becoming. The dialectical problem posed by the play can be stated in Eliot's terms: man must be both an individual and a member. If he is just an individual, the result tends toward anarchy; if he is only a member, the result tends toward communism. The essential problem then is one of liberty—the extremes of which are anarchy and tyranny—as the quoted passages by the Duke, Claudio, and Lucio make clear. The social answer is a society that allows maximum human freedom for the individual as member. The Shakespearean answer given in *Measure for Measure* may be said to be found in the family. And it is toward the family, an enlarged family, that the symbolism of the play moves.

Measure for Measure doesn't lie about the nature of life, about the huge difficulty of finding any kind of human solution to existence. It doesn't, for instance, say that we can truly live in this world by ignoring the problems of living. It doesn't say that we can do what we can get away with, with due regard for the policeman around the corner. It doesn't advocate "the stoical scheme of supplying our wants by lopping off our desires." The sides of the play are self-centeredness and sacrifice, vanity and love. The essential human problem rendered by the play is how man is to live, to be ruled, and to rule. And the enormously complex solution to this problem is the Shakespeare ethic of love and duty in operation.

II

The Duke and the Office of Duke

In I, 1, the Duke in his own person directs Angelo:

Hold therefore, Angelo—
In our remove be thou at full ourself.
Mortality and mercy in Vienna
Live in thy tongue and heart. Old Escalus,
Though first in question, is thy secondary.
Take thy commission.

Angelo will be the Duke. By only slightly changing the punctuation, we may read the third and fourth lines as indicating that mortality and mercy in Vienna live in Escalus' tongue and heart as well as in Angelo's tongue and heart, *or* rather than in Angelo's tongue and heart. If mercy lives in Escalus' heart, it is living there or living only there, for Escalus, as Angelo's secondary, is dependent upon Angelo and cannot himself grant mercy, at least cannot grant mercy to Claudio. First Escalus and then the Provost will unsuccessfully appeal to Angelo for Claudio's life. Mercy will depend on Isabella, Isabella aided by Lucio's insidious advice and with the good offices of the again-present Provost. Angelo is seduced by Isabella: he will decide to let mercy live, not because he feels for Claudio, but because he desires Isabella. Later, after his "fall," Angelo will be unmerciful, for he will then feel that his future depends on Claudio's death, on mortality.

Thus the third and fourth lines of the passage contain two sets of doubles—mortality and mercy, tongue and heart—and if it is said that the two lines squint (that is, may refer to either Angelo or Escalus or to both), we may suppose, as I have already suggested, that the first item of each pair applies to Angelo and that the second item of each pair applies to Escalus. Angelo has mortality and the tongue; Escalus has mercy and the heart. By leaving his role in Vienna, the Duke is giving mortality and the tongue to Angelo and thus making mercy and the heart, upon which human life depends, subservient to Angelo's will. Angelo is the master, the head here; he has not discovered his heart. "Take thy commission" may

refer to the commission given to Angelo *and* (if we say that
mortality and mercy are to live in Escalus' tongue and heart)
to the commission given to Escalus.[1]

The metrical line "Take thy commission" is completed by
Angelo's next words, "Now, good my lord." Angelo is of
course addressing the Duke, and the Duke is good here. The
commission is good here; the commission to Angelo *or* to
Escalus is good here. Perhaps we may also see *now,* the present,
as being good here. It is only after Angelo falls that his good
office can turn to evil uses. Angelo is authority and is the
dispenser of temporal justice. Further, then, we seem to be
given the distinction between the office and the person holding
the office, a tension between the man and the office he holds:
Angelo is tested in and by the office that the Duke has given
him. Escalus can make himself felt in special and in limited
situations, as with Elbow in II, 1.

In I, 2, Lucio and the gentlemen are introduced; Mistress
Overdone and Pompey are introduced; Claudio, Juliet, and
the Provost are introduced. The only figure of temporal authority is the Provost, and he is carrying out Angelo's orders, though
he doesn't believe that Claudio deserves to be punished. The
scene is filled with talk of sex and sin, of venereal disease,
persecution, and repression—lechery attending authority. In
I, 3, the Duke and Friar Thomas are seen; at the beginning
of I, 4, Isabella and Francisca, a nun, are introduced. After
the Duke puts on the habit of friar, Isabella is called away
from putting on the habit of sister. We understand that the
Duke has to become a brother and that Isabella has to be
Claudio's true sister if craft is to work against vice and if
the world is to be made secure. The Duke and Isabella will
become the true leaders in the world, its proper head and its
proper heart, its best husband and wife, and the world has
to be brought from vanity into true reality, into a recognition

---

[1] Miss Pope cites William Perkins' *Treatise on Christian Equity and Mod-
eration* as one of many authorities who distinguish two kinds of bad judges.
According to Perkins, one kind is made up of "such men, as by a certain
foolish kind of pity are so carried away, that would have nothing but
mercy, mercy . . ."; the other kind is made up of "such men as have
nothing in their mouths, but the *law*, the *law*: and *Justice, Justice* . . ."
(Pope, p. 74). Clearly an example of the first kind is Escalus; an example
of the second kind is Angelo.

of what being human means, before the Duke and Isabella can be what the world will demand that they become.

It may be said that in I, 2, the body presents itself, that in I, 3, the true head dons a religious mask, that in I, 4, the heart is called into the world, away from a religious sanctuary. Act II, 1, begins with Angelo, Escalus, and a Justice. The similarity of this character group to the character group in I, 1, allows us to imagine that in a manner of speaking the play is beginning again. Significant dramatic and poetic facts have been established, new characters have been introduced, and now, in II, 1, the play begins anew, with Angelo replacing in fact the Duke. Escalus has taken Angelo's place; the Justice has taken Escalus' place. In I, 1, the Duke, Angelo, Escalus are introduced; II, 1, begins with Angelo, Escalus, the Justice. Just as I, 1, ends with Angelo talking to Escalus, so II, 1, ends with Escalus talking to the Justice.

When Angelo as Duke is presented with a moral problem demanding a just decision, he listens to Elbow's mistakings, to Froth's flightiness, and to Pompey's skipping chatter, and then he gives the problem to Escalus, and he, Angelo, departs. Sin has been ignored; justice will be subverted; guile and selfishness determine the end. The major point is that in a manner of speaking Angelo is acting here the way the Duke must have acted in the past, as Duke. In other words, the "unplanned" conspiracy in II, 1, serves to explain why the Duke at the beginning of the play would feel that he should test the office of Duke. At the beginning of the play the world lacks effective leadership: the Duke feels that he hasn't provided successful leadership. Angelo's behavior in II, 1, seems to prove what the Duke at the moment knows: exercising human authority is difficult. In fact, then, in II, 1, we may be allowed to believe that if Isabella were not to come before Angelo, Angelo would in time be not much different as a ruler from the way the Duke was when he delivered the city to Angelo. An upright Angelo would come to feel the hopelessness of controlling an amoral constituency. Specifically, if there were no Isabella, the world would never become human.

Angelo leaves the Elbow-Froth-Pompey problem as a problem to Escalus. Angelo's tough justice is effective only when a "forgotten" law is enforced. Thus Claudio and Constable

Elbow are both related expressions of the inability of justice to operate with human effectiveness. Paradoxically, the complexity of the human problem as rendered by *Measure for Measure* is of a simple nature: "All difficulties are but easy when they are known." The essential problem is one of ignorance and selfishness. It is, however, difficult to sort out precise blame, to assess specific fault, for, in a seeming, uninstructed world, justice becomes a complex problem. Human beings are what they are. Elbow or Elbow's wife cannot be simply excused. From an enlightened viewpoint Claudio's guilt is quite excusable.

Thus in the middle of II, 1, the moral problem of the play is stated both in the simplest terms and as a kind of Chinese box, as a series of levels, or as an expanded list. The complex, symbolic problem is posed in realistic, human terms. Constable Elbow stands for simple justice; Escalus is now acting for and as Angelo here; Angelo, the nominal deputy, has left; the true Duke is acting as the Friar. Elbow has no wisdom. As moral considerations move away from Elbow or from simple justice, moral awareness becomes colder, though, of course, more encompassing and more philosophic. From some distance, the simple matter of the Elbow problem doesn't seem very important. But how truly meaningful justice is depends in part upon how able and how dispassionate simple justice is. A fool isn't the answer. A tyrant isn't the answer. Again, the relevant considerations concern the office and the person holding the office. And, in fact, any office depends upon the effectiveness of every other person and every other office. In II, 1, the problem of justice is realistically rendered by the case of Elbow-Elbow's absent wife-Froth-Pompey.

A Shakespeare play always demonstrates how real the problem of human justice is, and how ineffective, casual, and cruel human justice can easily become. The practical answer is mending, doing what can be done in order to make life better. A true world, a world of human values, a good world, depends upon continuous mending. This is the least man can do: it is what man owes to human life. Mending is determined by the individual's position (his office) and his ability: it requires someone who can really mend, and it relies upon a world that can be effectively mended. When Isabella first comes before the Duke in V, 1, she madly denounces Angelo. The Duke objects. She asks for pardon: "The phrase is to the matter." The Duke relies, "Mended again." Love and duty best mend.

In V, 2, of *Much Ado About Nothing,* after Beatrice and Benedick have wittily declared their love for each other, Benedick remarks: "Serve God, love me, and mend." First, Beatrice must serve something outside herself; then, she must love him; then, she must mend wrong, correct faults. To be meaningfully valuable, mending must be done because of faith and love: the world is mended to faith and love out of faith and love. A sense of duty and a feeling of love should direct mending. The best answer for a human society is, Shakespeare would seem to say, the philosopher-king *and* an instructed, corrected world, a world sanctified by marriage. The world needs a head, a heart, and creative imagination, and even these may not be enough. The usual world needs to be transformed, and in Shakespearean comedy it is transformed.

We simply assume that the Duke would see the larger significance of the Elbow case in II, 1, but even if he were to see it, he probably would act little differently from the way Angelo or Escalus does. What can be done? And, after all, prisoners were executed under the Duke's rule, too. The Duke knows the impossibility of human justice. In fact, Angelo's leaving the problem in II, 1, repeats or rehearses the Duke's different leaving in I, 1. The way Angelo behaves in II, 1, seems in part to be a statement of the way the Duke behaved before *Measure for Measure* begins. We may well believe that Escalus acts as the Duke would have acted: "Which is the wiser here? Justice or Iniquity?" Further and more important, we, the audience, have the advantage of knowing what Angelo and Escalus do not know: the Duke and Isabella have come back to the world. Thus the means of the answer to the riddle of the world are given. The answer needs to be found, and all of the characters have to be humanly brought to desire the answer.

In II, 1, the tongue and the heart are ineffective in every sense. At first the tongue is divorced from the heart. In IV, 3, the Duke hears an offstage voice say, "Peace ho, be here!" and he remarks, "The tongue of Isabel." By the end of the play Isabella, believing that her brother has been murdered by Angelo, can still kneel beside Mariana before the Duke and beg for mercy to Angelo. She can then best serve Mariana and can truly make the tongue serve the heart; precisely, she will beg that mercy be placed above mortality. Isabella's great act of Christian charity puts the seal on the secured world. In that Isabella is the tongue that is needed if the heart is to be expressed, Shakespeare is utilizing the conceit of the world as an ordered body. In this conceit Isabella is the tongue that can best express the deep human feeling of the discovered heart at the end of the play.[2]

In II, 1, when Angelo leaves the Elbow-Froth-Pompey problem, Escalus says, "Good morrow to your lordship." Apparently Angelo is to be distinguished from his lordship, Angelo from the Duke: because Angelo as Duke has failed his authority, his lordship is being bid farewell to, his being Duke is being bid farewell to. But in a deeper, stricter sense, the Duke's lordship is being awakened, is being bid good morrow to: "Good morrow to *your* lordship." Angelo's failure provides the way to the Duke's success. Angelo must fail so that the Duke can succeed. If *lord* is distinguished from *lordship,* the implication is that the lordship is going to be defined and that then the proper lord, who will be able to fill the office of lord, can be found or will be found. The problem at the beginning of the play is that the world has lost its meaning, and if the world is without meaning, lordship is meaningless. The answer will come after instruction and correction, when the world is again invested with meaning.

A human world needs complete human beings. Angelo must discover desire, must first become irresponsible, like Elbow, Froth, or Pompey; Isabella must become what she potentially is. The Duke has to recognize the extent of his obligation and then has to take back his proper role. Only then will a true, human society be realized. In a sense every movement is a movement into complexity. As the old law against fornication is enforced, Lucio is turned from being a loose-living pleasure-seeker into being a wicked tongue. The tension between words and deeds, between the name and the thing, is always relevant, as the action moves toward the dawn, to the city gate, into secure reality. Every movement is a movement into inclusiveness, for nothing is canceled: any new thing is accommodated and the end is thus made finer by that accommodation.

---

[2] See John L. Harrison, "The Convention of 'Heart' and 'Tongue' and the Meaning of *Measure for Measure,*" *Shakespeare Quarterly,* V (1954), 1-10.

III

The Duke On Stage and Off

In his excellent article Nevill Coghill maintains that *Measure for Measure* "shows a human world in an eternal situation, not a series of abstractions in a contrived predicament, like a Morality Play or like the comedies of Ben Jonson." In *Measure for Measure* human beings are tested. Mr. Coghill then goes on to say: "In *Measure for Measure* the reason for testing human beings is the one given in the Sermon on the Mount." The tests are made possible, directly or indirectly, by the Duke; moreover, this steward of this world must be instructed in the reality of his stewardship. Both the world and the Duke are instructed and brought to understanding. As the world tests the Duke, the Duke tests the world.[1] Structurally, III, 2, may be considered the scene designed to display the old Duke and what the office of Duke means.

Throughout III, 2, the Duke in his guise of Friar is on stage: other persons come and go, but the Duke remains on stage, as the visible brother and as the potential father. We, the audience, are meant to be exceptionally aware of the Duke's presence as Duke here, for in this scene he speaks the riddle and gives the long octosyllabic soliloquy. It is as if the forces released by the Duke's abdication of authority in I, 1, come into the open and are brought to the Duke as Friar in III, 2. The Duke is a seen but unseen presence: the other characters see him as Friar; we know him to be the Duke. In III, 2, the Duke and we are shown the difficulties attendant upon the

---

[1] "Angelo judges Claudio, Claudio and Lucio judge Isabella: Escalus judges Pompey, and so does Abhorson, from their different professional angles. But Pompey has also his profession with *its* point of view, and judges society from that; as Barnardine weighs human life by his own morose philosophy; while the Duke bustles around judging all and sundry—with the amount of success that usually attends one in a sweat to overtake his neglected business." (Sir Arthur Quiller-Couch, Introduction to the New Shakespeare Edition of *Measure for Measure*, Cambridge, 1922, pp. XXV-XXVI.)

Duke in his anomalous role as both brother and father. His complete progress is from seeming Duke to seeming Friar to real Duke.

Elbow, Pompey, and officers come onto the stage, for Pompey has been at last arrested as a bawd and a thief. Nothing is said about Froth or Elbow's wife, and Elbow is still constable, though Escalus was apparently going to find a replacement for him after speaking to Elbow in II, 1. In time under Angelo the world has become less frothy, clearer, naturally more just, though not necessarily better. The imposition of law, whether just or not, has simplified the problem, has destroyed the initial, "seeming" world. Angelo, as substitute Duke, as intransigent father, has had an effect.

The first words of III, 2, are by Elbow:

> Nay, if there be no remedy for it but that you
> will needs buy and sell men and women like
> beasts, we shall have all the world drink brown
> and white bastard.

Pompey has broken the law, but then, in a different sense, so has the Duke as Friar. A moment before, in III, 1, the Duke interfered with justice in order to save Claudio, to protect Isabella, to "advantage" Mariana. As a lawbreaker and as a bawd, Pompey (who in a double sense comes before the Duke here) is then a version of the Duke, a parody of the Duke. In other words, both the Duke and we are presented with a version of what the Friar's action has been and of what the Duke now is. Thus Elbow's initial lines implicate the Duke, for both Pompey and the Duke have been "caught" buying and selling men and women. We have just heard the Duke advising Isabella to give in to Angelo's importunity. That is to say, Pompey and the Duke are to be equated as bawds and then distinguished as being different kinds of bawds: unlike Pompey, the Duke "uses" men and women for their own good, for the world's good, as a remedy against vice.

When Lucio enters, the seedy Pompey begs his sometime friend to provide comfort and bail. Reflecting the new, ruthless world, Lucio brutally rejects Pompey: fellowship is accursed. We, the audience, are aware that the man who can best give comfort and bail is the Duke, that other, finer bawd, though neither Pompey nor Lucio knows that the Friar, that brother, can summon, if he wishes, temporal power to the secular world. Alone with the Friar, the blind Lucio abuses the absent Angelo and slanders the "absent" Duke. He is nasty to anyone who has been caught, and he is backbiting to those in authority. Lucio is no longer a willing messenger; he is not like the new Isabella. The world has not improved; the sore of corruption is open; Lucio is worse than ever. If Lucio is worse than ever, the Duke must become better than before. A bad father increases the value of a good brother; a bad brother makes a good father necessary. In the next scene, the beginning of the second half of the play, the Duke will come to the moated grange as a "man of comfort." Clearly, the human world needs something finer than a bawd, something finer than simple justice. Mercy is needed. The heart is needed. True relationships are needed. The answer waits. Here in III, 2, the Duke and his office are being tested. The Duke is on stage; the person holding the office of Duke, Angelo, is off stage.

At the beginning of the scene the Duke as Friar addresses Pompey, the bawd: he tells him to mend, and then he says, "Correction and instruction must both work / Ere this rude beast will profit." Lucio, who then enters, is, if anything, worse than the beast Pompey. Moreover, Lucio, the slanderer, is someone who will openly speak in a "safe" company of the Duke as a bawd. We are asked to see the Duke as being like Pompey, and then Lucio insists that the Duke has been like Pompey: "Yes, your beggar of fifty, and his use was to put a ducat in her clackdish; the Duke had crotchets in him. He would be drunk, too: that let me inform you." Lucio's calumny forces the Duke as Friar to defend himself as openly as his role permits him, and, when truth is discounted, the Duke admits to himself and to us that no man in authority can control vicious slander.

Significantly, then, Lucio's words of abuse to Pompey in the Duke's presence can be seen as being also applicable to the Duke, that other Pompey:

> What, is there none of Pygmalion's images, newly
> made woman, to be had now, for putting the hand
> in the pocket and extracting it clutched? What
> reply, ha? What sayest thou to this tune, matter

> and method? Is't not drowned i' the last rain, ha?
> What sayest thou, Trot? Is the world as it was,
> man? Which is the way? Is it sad, and few words?
> Or how? The trick of it?[a]

Both Pompey and the Duke can make no meaningful reply.
Though abusive in intent to Pompey and abusive by implication to the Duke as Friar, the answer that Lucio gives the
caught Pompey will be the same answer that the caught Duke
will be brought to accept, once the brutal world is reinvested
with proper awe: "You will turn good husband now, Pompey,
you will keep the house." Metaphorically, the house that
the Duke will come to keep will be that of Vienna.

After vicious Lucio leaves, Escalus, the Provost, Mistress Overdone, and officers enter. Apparently Lucio has supplied the
authorities with information that has brought about the arrest
of Mistress Overdone. The riddle upon which the wisdom of
the world runs was seen with Lucio and Pompey, with Lucio
and the Duke; it is now seen again, differently. For the first
time we hear of Kate Keepdown and of Lucio's bastard child
and of Mistress Overdone's service to that illicit family. Lucio
has even turned against those that he has used and those that
have served him and those that have depended upon him.
He wants to do no mending; he is only selfish and very vain.
Understandably, the enforcement of Angelo's laws has proven
effective: Pompey and Mistress Overdone did not reform and
were caught. And Lucio, the apostle of license, has become
the instrument of repressive justice. Under Angelo, Vienna
has become like a police state. To Lucio, Angelo is not human,
and Lucio intends to conform to the new master. The emphasis
in Angelo's world is on mortality, the lack of fellowship, the
absence of heart. Lucio and his actions in III, 2, brilliantly
express what Lucio perceives to be Angelo's world, a world
where understanding and mercy are unthinkable. Significantly,
Lucio causes the Duke to verbalize the riddle upon which the
wisdom of the world runs.

Three times during III, 2, the Duke is on the fluid Elizabethan stage alone: at the beginning; in the middle; at the
end. The Duke talks to Isabella; she leaves and the Duke

---

[a] "This tune" would seem to refer to the song, which will shortly be sung;
rain is of course also *reign,* and *ha* is *awe.*

is alone on stage for a moment before the new scene begins. At the end of III, 2, the Duke speaks his octosyllabic lines, and then Mariana and the boy appear on stage. On one side of the Duke in III, 2, is Isabella, at the end of III, 1; on the other side of the Duke in III, 2, are Mariana and the boy, in IV, 1. As a matter of fact the Duke speaks to himself and to us, the audience, four times during the scene: as Elbow and Pompey enter; right before Lucio enters; between the time that Lucio leaves and the time that Escalus, the Provost, and Mistress Overdone enter; at the end, before Mariana and the boy come on stage. Each of these four statements by the Duke functions as a choric comment on the action that has just occurred; moreover, each comment takes place as or just before a new character or characters appear on stage, so that the implications of each comment are at once extended on stage for us.

When Elbow and Pompey come on stage and after Elbow's initial words, the Duke remarks to himself:

Oh heavens! What stuff is here?

Just before Lucio enters, the Duke comments:

That we were all, as some would seem to be,
From our faults, as faults from seeming, free!

After Lucio departs, the Duke speaks to himself:

No might nor greatness in mortality
Can censure 'scape, back-wounding calumny
The whitest virtue strikes. What king so strong
Can tie the gall up in the slanderous tongue?
But who comes here?

At the end of the scene the Duke begins the twenty-two-line speech to himself in this way:

He who the sword of Heaven will bear
Should be as holy as severe.

These four statements then mark stages in the development of the Duke's understanding of his public self. After the Duke is instructed here and instructs us here, the second half of the play may begin.

When Escalus enters with his group, we, if not the Duke, may be expected to see Escalus as still holding his commission of mercy, and we may see Mistress Overdone, who mentions

Kate Keepdown and the child, as being an indication of the play's answer, as being the imaged "lost" family, as being the means of tying the gall up in the slanderous tongue. The family still lacks a father, the head, the master. The father, the ruler capable of tying up gall, must be holy and severe. Having accepted this fact, the Duke will silence Lucio at the very end of the play. After the enlarged family has been established, when everyone else has explicitly accepted the Duke as the rightful father, gall will be tied up. Again, Shakespeare seems to insist that the disguised Duke must be made to feel and thus to understand the intransigence of being a ruler, the meaning of might and mortality. Thus, again, the exceptional value to the Duke of Lucio's vicious slander is that by means of it, the Duke is given a shocking view of himself and of his lordship and a rendering of the world to which Angelo now subscribes.[3] And the Duke's growing understanding is a means of expressing our increased understanding.

After Lucio leaves and after the Duke gives the riddle upon which the wisdom of the world runs, Escalus describes the disposition of the Duke as a person who "contended especially to know himself." But in his ignorance Escalus sees Angelo as Justice, and he sees the Duke as only a Friar:

> You have paid the Heavens your function, and the
> prisoner the very debt of your calling. I have
> labored for the poor gentleman to the extremest
> shore of my modesty. But my brother Justice have
> I found so severe that he hath forced me to tell
> him he is indeed Justice.

The absent Angelo stands for three different aspects of justice: to Pompey he is father justice; to Escalus he is brother justice; to the Duke he is vain justice. Three Angelos and three aspects of justice are being implicitly tested. But, beyond that, at the moment, the world of Vienna is being tested by and in love and duty. Again, the world must be instructed by and in the ethic of love and duty. A bawd can only bring a man and a

---

[3] Speaking of Lucio's bringing Isabella from the convent in I, 4, J. W. Lever remarks, "In reality it is Lucio, not Escalus or Angelo, who serves here as the Duke's true deputy" (Lever, p. XCVI). This insightful suggestion seems useful in III, 2, where in a sense Angelo, Escalus, the Provost, and Lucio may be seen as deputies of the Duke.

woman together: his office both is made possible by and is limited by love and duty.

Lucio's "Why, what a ruthless thing is this in him, for the rebellion of a codpiece to take away the life of a man!" Of course Lucio is referring to Claudio and the rebellion of his codpiece. The Duke and we know, though Lucio does not, that Angelo's codpiece has also rebelled. In fact, Lucio's flinty attitude is an expression of what he takes to be Angelo's attitude. The rebellion of his codpiece will make Angelo ruthless, something that the Duke does not expect. Angelo will then break his hollow word and insist upon Claudio's death. Paradoxically, the secure family of the end will result from this rebellion; the change in Angelo and how the Duke uses this change will serve to push down not only Angelo but also Lucio: Lucio will become a burr that will stick to the Friar before he is made by the Duke an unwilling husband.

In a manner of speaking, III, 2, presents Lucio's Angelo, the Duke's Angelo, Mariana's Angelo, though Mariana and thus her Angelo have not yet been actually presented on stage. In a comparable way, Lucio's Duke is not the true Duke, is not the Duke as Friar, is not Escalus' Friar: the true, realized Duke will come forth at the end, when the world has changed, when the world is ready for the true Duke to emerge. *Measure for Measure* needs the proper head, the proper heart, the proper hands, a human world, a world of meaningful relationships. And human involvement is the means by which the real world is brought to light.

At the end of III, 1, Isabella leaves the Duke in order to go, as the Duke has requested, to Angelo; in IV, 1, Isabella comes to the Duke and Mariana from seeing Angelo. So while we watch the others in III, 2, Isabella is busy elsewhere. It would seem clear then that the action of III, 2, can be taken as a correlative to what is happening off stage and that the structure of III, 2, is, at least in part, determined by the off-stage correlative action. Hence, the middle of III, 2, when Lucio and the Duke are alone together on stage, is apparently meant to be the exact time that Isabella is with Angelo alone. Angelo's attitude *at the moment* is manifested to us, if not to the Duke, by Lucio's slander. What Lucio and the Duke say is a kind of index to what Isabella and Angelo are *at the moment* saying. At this stage of the action, Lucio has come to be the Duke's proper antagonist, just as Angelo has come to be Isabella's proper antagonist. As we watch Lucio and the Duke, we are supposed to think of Isabella and Angelo, to remember Isabella and Angelo, to remember that both of them are "acting out" the Duke's orders.

Perhaps we are also meant to see further, to see that Lucio has here picked up the brutal manner to a brother, the manner that Isabella gave up in III, 1, when she acceded to the Friar's advice: after being cruel to Claudio, Isabella obeys the Friar. The resultant ironies from the various equations are multiple but evident. Angelo is and is not the Duke; Lucio is and is not Isabella; Isabella is and is not a victim; the Duke is and is not the Friar. We, the audience, see the effects of Lucio-Isabella on the Duke-Angelo. Both the Duke and Angelo are "visibly" changed by what they hear. In this way both the Duke and Angelo are given a view of themselves and their world that is at once distorted and true. If we will only see and imagine, we are being given a rendering of that which is a complex truth.

Perhaps the subsuming notion should be expressed in a different way. Lucio's abuse of Angelo and of the Duke is qualified by our listening to the Duke's *true voice* here and by our imagining the correlative, offstage action. When Lucio-Isabella leave, and when Escalus brings his group on stage, we are meant to see Mistress Overdone as being a kind of parody of Isabella; for Isabella has just agreed to sell herself to Angelo. If Mistress Overdone is a kind of diminished expression of Isabella, then Kate Keepdown stands for Mariana, and the child signifies the child that will be the product of the assignation in the garden house. Just as Mariana has not yet been presented, so Kate and the child are mentioned but not presented. In this way Escalus and the Provost—the good servants—"bring" the answer onto the stage for us to imaginatively perceive it.

Finally, then, Shakespeare seems to be insisting that III, 2, be used as a key to understanding the implications of the dramatic action: the scene renders the danger to which the women's good intentions and the men's selfish concerns have brought the world. Fed by good intentions, selfish concerns have brought the world to this precarious place. Recognizing, first, the dismal truth concerning the wisdom of the world, the Duke, the absent father and the present brother, accepts by implication and then by open admission the necessity of using craft. But craft isn't enough. A good counselor is at the whim of the person who holds power and authority. Either he must stop being a good counselor, or he must get higher power or other authority. The Duke as Friar is willing now to use subversive means in order to regain the authority nominally held by Angelo. As the true Duke rises (and is made to rise) within the Friar's costume, so Angelo will subside into being a man. In III, 2, the three main stages of the Duke's progress are indicated: Brother, Father, Bearer of the Sword of Heaven.

IV

"Remember Now My Brother"

In IV, 1, after Isabella has told Mariana the story, she returns with Mariana and makes this statement:

> Little have you to say
> When you depart from him, but, soft and low,
> "Remember now my brother."

The comment is, first of all and clearly, addressed to Mariana. But since the Friar has just spoken to Isabella, the advice may be taken as being addressed to the Friar, to the Duke as Friar. There is then an initial complexity concerning the identity of the *you*. Names are not given.

In the night, Angelo will of course think that it is Isabella that speaks the directed words and that he is being reminded to remember his promise concerning Claudio. But since the "known" person will really be Mariana, we are given to understand that the brother that Mariana must mean is Frederick, the great soldier, whose death at sea prompted Angelo to break off the engagement to Mariana. In another, deeper sense, the brother is the Friar, the visible, religious brother whose advice Isabella and Mariana are here preparing to carry out. The Duke as Friar is a substitute and a deputy for Claudio and for Frederick: he is a brother to Isabella and a brother to Mariana. Angelo should remember the first two brothers, but it is this third brother that Angelo should always remember, for this brother is his absent lord, the master he is the surrogate for. We are meant to perceive three brothers that Angelo ought to remember: Frederick, Claudio, the Duke; a past brother, a present brother, a masquerading, future brother.

It is possible to read "my brother" as being in direct address: in that Mariana will keep the assignation, both Isabella and Mariana are involving themselves in guilt as sisters and are addressing Angelo as their brother in guilt, as if the assignation is not simply adulterous but also incestuous. If *now* is emphasized, the implication is that the conditions have been met by

Isabella through Mariana: "'Remember *now*, my brother.'" *Now* it is Angelo's turn to remember. But *now* also indicates that it is the committed sexual intrigue that he should remember. Moreover, it is this bargain—and by implication that other bargain with Frederick and that other bargain with the Duke —that he shouldn't forget, as he has or soon will. Further, Angelo is ironically being instructed to remember what he does not know, the good duplicity—the conspiracy of the Duke, Isabella, Mariana—that has just caught him.

We readily see the ways that Angelo and Claudio and the Duke are alike. At the end of the play the Duke will specifically refer to Claudio as his brother. And if "my brother" is seen as being in direct address, we may see Claudio or the Duke as being that brother: as we can see, the Friar—the Duke as brother—is on the stage at this moment. He is the brother being addressed at the moment, and the Duke is being asked to remember *now* what *he* is doing. The Duke is then also being admonished to remember what will happen in the garden house, the intrigue that he is largely responsible for. The Duke as Friar has deeply implicated himself in the affairs of others: he may not now forget that. In III, I, Isabella said to Claudio, "Is't not a kind of incest, to take life / From thine own sister's shame?" The incest will be controlled and the shame will be conditioned by the "brotherly" acts of Claudio, of Angelo, and of the Duke.

"Remember" says what it literally means: Angelo is being told to *re-member* the body, the family, mercy and justice, the public demands and the private needs. In addition, he is being told to re-member *now*, to join *now* with the past—both his personal past and the Duke's public past—to join *now*, the present, with the future. Angelo will try to wipe out the deed, to erase it, and it will be the function of these three good conspirators to keep the "act" alive, to use it to re-member the world at the end of the play. More and more, re-membering will depend upon the Duke, who will perforce have to reassume his proper role as the viable head in order to continue to secure the mended world.

"Soft and low," Isabella's advice to Mariana, is designed to prevent Angelo from distinguishing the servant from the maid, Mariana from Isabella: the deception is necessary in order for the trick to be accomplished. The words of advice thus serve to reinforce the reciprocal relationship of Isabella and Mariana: Isabella will act as Mariana's "low" servant, just as Mariana, Isabella's substitute, will act as the "soft and low" savior of Frederick, Claudio, Isabella, herself, Angelo, and the Duke. Mariana is then, in a sense, Isabella; and "soft and low" describes what Mariana's behavior will be in the night. The words also document the growing humanization of Isabella, how softness and lowness are now, at this moment, changing her from the self-righteous, unbending sister she intended to be at the beginning to the loving wife she will surely become after the play has ended.

"Fear me not"—Mariana's three-word answer to Isabella's advice—can be seen as extending Isabella's " 'Remember now my brother' ": in fact, Mariana's three words complete the metrical line. Mariana gives her assurance that she will do what she must for the Duke as Friar, for Isabella, for Claudio, for herself, and, finally, for Angelo. "Fear me not" can be seen as a further admonition to Angelo and, by extension, to each of the other brothers: Remember *and* fear me not. What should be remembered and re-membered is not fearing "me." As we have seen, the pronouns *my* and *me* in the full line can be taken as applying to any of a series of characters. There is no cause for fear: what the conspirators are doing will help to insure the safety of all. They are doing what is necessary to prevent Angelo from sinning so that he and, by extension, the whole world will be saved. An unchecked Angelo would bring the whole world down. The world will be saved by trickery and through a snare, for vice here demands that craft be employed. And meaningful craft depends finally upon the Duke.

"Nor, gentle Daughter, fear you not at all." The Duke's next words, after Mariana's three-word addition to Isabella's advice, refer to Mariana as his daughter, his obedient "child." The Duke as apparent brother and as real father underwrites Mariana's admonition to "fear me not." We are meant to perceive that this Friar has some power to control evil and fear. In IV, 3, the Duke's first words to Isabella, right before he tells her that Angelo has had Claudio killed, will be to call her daughter. Isabella moves from being a sister to being an accepted wife. Thus the father-child relationships emerge out of the elaborate brother-brother and brother-sister relationships that are patently in IV, 1. Again, the principal symbolic movement of the play is toward the established and enlarged family. The Duke will end as brother, father, husband: he will end his symbolic movement with the establishment of all three roles.

The boy in IV, 1, who sings the song and then disappears, may, like the boy in *Henry IV, 11* or the boy in *Henry V*, represent the simple servant as well as representing the future, the generation to which the world will be delivered. Singing the song, the boy enters the play with Mariana. The song seems to depend upon him, as if he is needed for the poetic idea of the song to be transmitted to us. In III, 2, we hear about Kate and her boy; at the beginning of IV, 1, we see Mariana and a boy. In a metaphoric sense the boy on stage is Kate's child and even, in time, in the future, a representation of Mariana's child by Angelo. Mariana and the boy are a kind of verification of desperation and of a desperate need. The woman and the child need a husband and a father. Though the notion need not be insisted upon, perhaps the nameless boy was the same boy who played Isabella on the stage (as if the audience were meant to see that the same boy was playing both roles), for the boy's place on stage is soon taken by Isabella: he departs and then Isabella enters. She takes over the boy's service in that she will be the means of stilling Mariana's "brawling discontent."

The boy serves Mariana by singing to her about her impossible position; Isabella will serve Mariana by providing a way toward what Mariana desires. And since the Duke will be also serving Mariana, we may see the singing boy as being a metaphoric version of the Duke. Moreover, in time, the Duke's kisses will bring a gain for Isabella. Isabella now tells the Duke, "For I have made him know / I have a servant comes with me along." Of course we know that the servant will be Mariana: Angelo must not be allowed to question the presence of two persons. But since Mariana will take Isabella's place with Angelo, it is Isabella who, both really and metaphorically, will be the servant. And insofar as Isabella and Mariana are working with the Friar to control Angelo's vice, we may say that Isabella is symbolically bringing the Duke—the good servant, the servant of good—along with her to Angelo.

In IV, 1, the Duke, Isabella, and Mariana may be said to represent the head, the heart, and the hand—one of Shakespeare's major configurations for presenting order. The Duke offers the solution; Isabella represents feeling or is the cause of feeling; Mariana is the instrument of the head (the Duke) that has been informed by the heart (Isabella). After the head and the heart have been found, the hand is needed. Here, at this stage of the play, the three parts, though present, are, in one way or another, not what they potentially are: the disguised head asks the discarded hand to operate as the desired heart. All three act the way they do because of the demands of craft. The head, the heart, and the hand are working in the dark and are moving toward a serviceable end, but an end that can be modified or even perverted by Angelo, the deputized head. Now the undeniable fact is that Angelo's actions after the assignation in the garden house will make the end finer and better than it would be if the Duke's craft were to simply prevail. The true head, heart, and hand will realize a true world.

The releasing of love will gain the world; the difficulty is that at the beginning of IV, 1, love is still sealed in vain:

> Take, O, take those lips away
>   That so sweetly were forsworn;
> And those eyes, the break of day,
>   Lights that do mislead the morn.
> But my kisses bring again, bring again,
> Seals of love, but sealed in vain, sealed in vain.

A sententious, masquerading Duke gives way to a singing boy. The rest of the play will demonstrate how the gain brought by kisses can lead to a love that will not be only vain or only in vain. The Duke must be taught the intransigence of desire; he must be taught by the heart. That is to say, the song can refer to the Duke's lips, to his eyes, to his lights. We have just heard him and seen him. And the Duke's intentions at the end of III, 2, are not heartfelt. Or the gain is to be found after Mariana gets back her old kisses, after that human miracle. For Angelo's kisses in the night will be the wrong expression of his true desire. While the song is being sung, the Duke is off stage; the Duke then does not hear the wisdom expressed by the song. We do. Like Angelo, the Duke does what he feels he must do, but the consequences of his action will lead him to the realization that he must, like Angelo again, do more than he is now willing to do. He must submit himself to the exigencies of a greater need. In other words, the truth is that the Duke must be brought by the heart to accept the peccant Angelo as his brother: " 'Remember now my brother.' " A singing boy leads us to the answer; a remembered brother leads the Duke to the answer.

In *Hamlet* the climax is the killing of Polonius; in *King Lear* it is the putting out of Gloucester's eyes; in *Measure for Measure* it is Isabella's capitulation to Angelo's importunity. Each climax comes in the last scene of Act III; though Isabella's actual agreement to meet Angelo in the garden is not presented, she does so, as we have seen, while other action is taking place on stage. At the beginning of Act IV, Hamlet, now a murderer, meets the murderer Claudius on different terms; Edgar, the outcast, discovers his blinded father, who has been seeking his life; Isabella meets Mariana and then they go to Angelo. Though *Measure for Measure* is a comedy and thus disaster is avoided, the poetic strategy is the same in that at this stage of the action in each play, forces are balanced, and the end is determined and insured. Hamlet and Claudius have to kill each other; Edgar begins to actually serve his father and ultimately himself; Isabella begins to serve the Duke and ultimately herself. In each play the past and the future impinge upon the present, and that impingement is rendered most precisely at the end of Act III and at the beginning of Act IV.

Shakespeare always seems to emphasize that human existence is conditioned by nature or what life essentially is; by time; by fortune or chance; by wit or man's ability to perceive and reason; and by necessity or that which has to be done: nature, time, fortune, wit, necessity. Throughout *Measure for Measure* these conditions operate, and in IV, 1, all five conditions gather to a head. The best human answer is, again, given us in the song: the seals of vanity must be broken; selfishness must be controlled; the world must be invested with love. The rest of the play shows us the world working out its salvation. The concord at the end is earned and won and—because the play is a comedy—given.

V

The Changed World

The first sixty-six lines of the next scene, IV, 2, constitute a parody of IV, 1: in effect, this part of the scene presents a version of IV, 1, the action in a different key. In other words, the action at the beginning of IV, 2, renders a kind of diminished parallel to the action in IV, 1, and, really, extends the thematic implications of the scene that presents the Duke, Isabella, and Mariana together. Just as the Duke, Isabella, and Mariana are caught by Angelo's sin and are brought by Angelo to act in concert, so the Provost, Abhorson, and Pompey are caught by the prison needs imposed by Angelo. Abhorson, like Isabella, needs help; the responsible Provost, like the Duke, enlists the services of Pompey in order to correct Claudio, who is of course to be compared with Angelo. The Provost is then a diminished version of the Duke; Abhorson is a diminished version of Isabella; Pompey is a diminished version of Mariana.

After the assignation, Angelo will believe that he is in something like Claudio's position, but of course Angelo means to control his destiny: he is powerful, callous, deadly. Angelo thinks he can use his power as Duke in order to prevent his being caught, as Claudio was caught. Though he doesn't realize it, Angelo *is being put* more precisely in Claudio's position than he would otherwise be. He thinks he has used Isabella; we know that Mariana has been enabled to be used and thus to win him. Angelo's behavior with Mariana is only in the present a more brutal version of Claudio's behavior with Juliet in the past, and he, like Claudio, is now caught by authority. Claudio is powerless; Angelo is on his way toward becoming powerless. As Angelo moves down (is moved down) to Claudio, the Duke moves back to power. The Duke must reassume his authority in order to avoid a disaster, and Angelo is the person from whom the Duke must take this authority.

It is, I think, a useful and meaningful comment to maintain that a Shakespeare play begins again in Act IV and that Shakespeare intends us to ponder the ways that the fourth act is like the first act. In other words, it seems to be a Shakespearean strategy that Act IV deliberately uses Act I. The play begins again, but with a real difference. Parallels and contrasts between Acts I and IV are meant to be perceived. Then the thematic, symbolic advancement of Act IV from Act I is meant to be understood. Perhaps the basic strategy may be seen most clearly in *Richard II*: I, 1, presents a ritual with Richard as king; IV, 1, is another ritual, but now Bolingbroke is king. In I, 1, of *Measure for Measure* the Duke submits his responsibility to Angelo and Escalus; in IV, 1, the Duke as Friar submits the moral problem to the good offices of Isabella and Mariana. Act IV begins after the initial, seeming world of Act I has become real. Initially, Mariana and Isabella were unrecognized sources of justice and mercy. The major point would seem to be this: now that the world is in touch with reality and truth, the play begins anew.

The Duke is the proper head, Isabella is the proper heart, the Provost is a proper hand, and it is toward the establishment of proper relationships that the play moves. At the end of IV, 2, the Duke tells the Provost, "Look, the unfolding star calls up the shepherd" and "Come away, it is almost clear dawn." And then Pompey comes on stage alone, to begin IV, 3: he delivers a twenty-two-line soliloquy. The new Pompey is as well acquainted in prison as he was in Mistress Overdone's own house: he mentions ten of her old customers and says that forty more of them are now in prison. In other words, the prison has taken the place of Mistress Overdone's house. In that she was sent to prison in III, 2, the prison is now her house. Pompey is at home, and he is helping to keep the house. What Lucio said to Pompey in III, 2, is now then true: "Commend me to the prison, Pompey. You will turn good husband now, Pompey, you will keep the house." If Pompey is now keeping the house in one sense, the Provost and the Duke are keeping it in another sense. Even the wicked bawd, Pompey, has metaphorically entered the service of the Duke.

At the beginning of IV, 2, in answer to the Provost's "Come hither, sirrah. Can you cut off a man's head?" Pompey answers,

"If the man be a bachelor, sir, I can. But if he be a married man, he's his wife's head, and I can never cut off a woman's head." Head-heart is thus imagistically an expression of husband-wife. The image of the family extends the image of the body. Out of the body comes the family. One trope expresses the other. Though the body will become sick and the family may dissolve, the notion of the healthy body and the idea of a true family provide the best, and perhaps the only, security in a Shakespeare play. Insofar as Claudio is Juliet's publicly recognized betrothed, he will not have his head cut off by Pompey.[1] Further, Pompey's lines assure us that by keeping the assignation, Angelo is insuring his proper marriage to Mariana. After the bed trick, Mariana-Angelo will be like Juliet-Claudio, and, again, we are here meant to understand that the intrigue of IV, 1, in fact saves Angelo. He must be made his wife's head: he will be a brother, a husband, a father. Claudio will be a brother, a husband, a father. The Duke will be a brother, a husband, a father.

The Provost's remark "The one has my pity, not a jot the other, / Being a murderer, though he were my brother" has reference to Claudio and Barnardine, but since Abhorson and Pompey have just left the stage, the lines would seem to refer also to them. Or, since the Provost's remark does not use names, we may be expected to supply them. Who is the murderer? Who is the brother? In effect then two pairs or two doubles are presented, and we are, I think, meant to identify the doubles in various ways and then to distinguish them in various ways—Claudio and Barnardine, Abhorson and Pompey. Claudio and Abhorson seem morally better than Barnardine and Pompey. Further, a notation about brotherhood is given, a qualification

---

[1] Ernest Schanzer makes a significant observation about the Claudio-Juliet-Isabella imbroglio: "The apparent contradiction between Isabel's condemnation of her brother's offence and her ready connivance in what would appear to be an identical transgression on the part of Mariana has often worried commentators. . . . Isabel appears to be ignorant throughout of her brother's marriage contract. . . . But why did Shakespeare choose to keep Isabel ignorant of the marriage-contract? Because had she known of it her entire plea before Angelo would have been different, an appeal to equity rather than to mercy." (Ernest Schanzer, *The Problem Plays of Shakespeare* (London, 1963), p. 110.) Incidentally, in the play the Duke tells Isabella about Mariana: "She should this Angelo have married, was affianced to her by oath, and the nuptial appointed."

about brotherhood is given: pity is not extended by the Provost to a murderous brother. The extensive Biblical imagery in the play would seem to suggest that *the* murderer is Cain and that *the* brother is Abel. In the Bible, Cain is cast out but not destroyed; in *Measure for Measure* the murder of a brother is prevented.

In the Folio, Pompey speaks the following lines, although the lines are usually now given to Abhorson:

> Every true man's apparel fits your thief. If it
> be too little for your thief, your true man
> thinks it big enough; if it be too big for your thief,
> your thief thinks it little enough. So every true
> man's apparel fits your thief.

This riddle is comparable to the Duke's riddle in III, 2. A hangman and a bawd are talking, and the conversation concerns Pompey's service to Abhorson, whether the bawd will serve the hangman. Traditionally, the hangman gets the hanged man's apparel: the clothing of the victim passes to the hangman, and since Pompey agrees to become a hangman, a bawd can become a hangman and can then be the recipient of the true man's apparel and can then "become" that true man. The doomed man here is either Claudio or Barnardine.

Specifically, the thief is a stealer of apparel. The true man's clothing may or may not fit the thief, but any stolen clothing will "fit" the thief. If the apparel does really fit the thief, the thief will look like the true man. In appearance the thief will be the true man. In the play the character most clearly wearing unsuitable apparel is the Duke, as if the Duke too is a kind of thief.[2] Primarily, of course, in wearing the Duke's apparel (whether the apparel fits or not), Angelo is the thief and the Duke is the true man. Again, as we have seen, when the Provost says "The one has my pity, not a jot the other," he is specifically referring to Claudio and Barnardine, but the reference may also be to Abhorson and Pompey, who have just

---

[2] The Folio text does not mention costume. Eileen Mackay avers that Isabella first comes on stage in plain clothes in IV, 1; before that, she is in the traditional nun's habit. According to Mrs. Mackay, it would be redundant for Isabella to be wearing the nun's habit at the end of the play. (Eileen Mackay, "*Measure for Measure,*" *Shakespeare Quarterly,* XIV (1963), 112.) As a person who changes costume, Isabella is a "stealer of apparel."

left the stage. Thus, the Duke, Claudio, and Abhorson may be seen as true men; Angelo, Barnardine, and Pompey may be seen as thieves.

In other words, in a few lines we hear talk of a true man and a thief, and we see a hangman and a bawd, and then the Provost speaks of a brother and a murderer. Roles are readily assigned: *the* true man is the Duke; *the* thief is Angelo; *the* hangman is Abhorson; *the* bawd is Pompey; *the* brother is Claudio; *the* murderer is Barnardine. In addition, a series of relationships is indicated: between true man and thief, between hangman and bawd, between a brother and a murderer. The terms may signify roles or stages that a character passes through. For example, Angelo goes from being a true man, to being a thief, to being a hangman, to being a bawd, to being a brother, to being a murderer. For it is in this scene that the Provost receives a letter from Angelo directing him to have Claudio executed by four o'clock.[3]

In this scene then, we are meant to perceive a statement of what the Duke's service has been and of what it will be. The Duke goes from stealing from Angelo (a true man), to serving Angelo (a hangman), to saving Angelo (a murderer). The Duke acts as a thief, a bawd, a brother. Further, all six roles accrue to the Duke at the end of V, 1, where the unhooded, acknowledged father is still wearing the garb of Friar. Though, as I have tried to suggest, the function of these terms must be dealt with in a variety of ways, we may subsume these ways by stating that the three pairs of terms present three stages in the symbolic action of the total play: true man-thief; hangman-bawd; brother-murderer.

Except for the Duke as Friar, the characters who will most effect the outcome are not on stage in IV, 2. Again, the Provost is an exponent of justice and is thus an exponent of the Duke or Angelo. It may then be said that Pompey is an exponent of Mariana and that Abhorson is an exponent of Isabella. Pompey will serve Abhorson, just as Mariana will serve Isabella. But, however the characters are taken, it seems true to say that each character who belongs in the prison renders the lowest moral possibilities of the more important characters

---

[3] Time is excellently treated by J. W. Lever, pp. XIV-XVII.

outside the prison. If, for example, Isabella were really to enter the cloister of Saint Clare, she would then become a kind of Abhorson, a servant of that place.

Moreover, just as III, 2, is the dramatic equivalent of Isabella's surrender to Angelo, so the beginning of IV, 2, is the dramatic equivalent of what is taking place in the garden. We perceive that the action in the prison is a reduced, brutal version of what is taking place in the dark in the garden house: this brutal prison scene is in actuality a dramatic statement of the surrender of Isabella-Mariana. We do not see Barnardine, though we hear about him. Like Angelo, Barnardine is off stage. When we see Claudio and hear about Barnardine, we are in essence seeing Claudio and hearing about Angelo, for Angelo is at that time turning himself into a Barnardine, a man who cares not at all for human life. After Angelo has fallen, he is willing to disregard any human value in order to seem to be what he was: he intends to brutally, selfishly mend. He puts himself above his office. Barnardine will appear in person before Angelo is seen again.

In *Othello,* which was written about the same time as *Measure for Measure,* as soon as Othello believes that Desdemona is a prostitute, Bianca is introduced. Bianca is a kind of actualization of what Desdemona has come to be in her husband's mind. Othello believes that his wife is a whore, and Bianca appears. Bianca is then another Desdemona, and she is then a kind of dramatic proof that Desdemona is not a whore: the role that Iago creates in Othello's mind is filled by the new character, Bianca. In *Measure for Measure* Shakespeare seems to be using this same strategic device: Barnardine is a kind of proof that Angelo is not a faithless murderer. Barnardine is what Angelo thinks that he, Angelo, has become. Or Barnardine fills a role that the instruments of good have created: conspiracy prevents Angelo from filling the role, and Barnardine is dramatic proof that Angelo is saved.

"He is coming, sir, he is coming, I hear his straw rustle." Pompey is referring to Barnardine (and thus to Angelo); however, I should like to suggest that Shakespeare is also alluding to the coming of Christ. In fact, the true man-thief riddle at the beginning of the prior scene may be an allusion to the Crucifixion. What the initial world of *Measure for Measure* desperately needs, as some excellent critics of the play have indicated, is the lesson of the Sermon on the Mount: the new world is realized in the second half of the play. The metaphoric coming forth or bringing forth of Christ depends on a blind, loveless world. And Barnardine enters the play as a kind of parody of Christ, the opposite of Christ: he is like Barabbas. In any case, Mariana precedes Barnardine *and* Christ: first, Mariana; then, Barnardine and, metaphorically, Christ. The initial world of the play needs the New Lesson of Love, and the second half of the play finds Love in the world, invests the world with true love. A character "dies" so that another may live. One person sacrifices himself for another. Yet in that the end of the play is safe and secure, the need for Christ is resolved happily.

Here, in IV, 2, of *Measure for Measure,* after Claudio enters, knocking is heard; after the Duke enters, knocking is heard twice more. The insistent noise distracts the characters and reminds us that something is wrong. It is as if Claudio is attended by some noise and as if the Duke is attended by more noise. After the first knocking, the Provost says, "Heaven give your spirits comfort." After the third knocking, the Duke comments, "That spirit's possessed with haste / That wounds the unsisting postern with these strokes." An uneasy spirit would seem to want to break in. When knocking is employed in *Henry IV, 1, Henry IV, 11, Troilus and Cressida, Othello,* and *Macbeth,* the intent is to render authority, force, power, some outside, new element that insists upon making itself felt. In *Measure for Measure* the first knocking may be seen as Angelo's desperate penetration of Mariana, the second knocking as Angelo's feeling of guilt, and the third knocking as Angelo's decision to murder Claudio. At least the three noises may be meant to signify the destruction of Isabella-Mariana, the destruction of Claudio, the destruction of Angelo.

Claudio and Barnardine have been summoned. Claudio comes onto the stage, and then knocking is heard: Claudio says that Barnardine will not awaken, and then knocking is heard. It is as if the intent of the knocking is to awaken Barnardine. If so, Barnardine may be expected to appear on stage. He doesn't. Instead, the Duke appears. If the Duke hasn't heard the knocking, Barnardine certainly hasn't. The Duke remarks, "The best and wholesomest spirits of the night / Envelop you, good Provost!" Thus heard spirits and unheard spirits are present, good spirits and bad spirits. We see Claudio and the Duke; we are meant to be reminded of Barnardine and Angelo. Perhaps unheard spirits must be heard, the spirits of evil must be turned to good. Again, Barnardine is expected, and the good Friar comes forth, the servant of good. *Night* in the Duke's line is perhaps to be seen as *knight:* it is Isabella as the knight of good, as the Provost of good, that will envelop destruction and bring Angelo to salvation.

The Provost and Claudio hear the first knocking; the Provost and the Duke hear the second knocking; the Duke hears the third knocking. The movement is toward the Duke's hearing the knocking alone. Knocking indicates first to the Provost and then to the Duke that the gate to Hell is opening. We may say, I think, that Claudio and the Provost represent the hands, instruments, and that the Duke represents the head, authority. The hand and the head hear the heart and then the head alone hears the heart. The symbolic action comes down to that, the heart making itself felt directly upon the head. The implicit, elaborate conceit seems to work from the notion that the prison is the body: first the body; then the hands; then the head. The responsibility is finally the head's. The last knocking comes when the Duke is alone. His response is, "How now! What noise?" A way must be found.

Salvation depends upon Isabella, the heart. Until the heart is made an active, useful force for good, there can be no true salvation. In II, 2, during Isabella's first interview with Angelo, he asks her why she has been putting these wise sayings upon him, and she replies:

> Because authority, though it err like others,
> Hath yet a kind of medicine in itself
> That skins the vice o' the top. Go to your bosom,
> Knock there, and ask your heart what it doth know
> That's like my brother's fault. If it confess
> A natural guiltiness such as is his,
> Let it not sound a thought upon your tongue
> Against my brother's life.
>
> *Angelo.* [*aside*] She speaks, and 'tis
> Such sense that my sense breeds with it.

As his aside indicates, it is this speech of Isabella's that seduces Angelo, that prompts desire in him. We can perhaps say that, for the first time, Angelo's heart is here truly moved. He feels what Claudio once felt before the seduction of Juliet, as if Angelo is now, at the moment, for the first time, humanly like Claudio, for Angelo never desired Mariana. Until he gives in to feeling, Angelo is not human. In retrospect from IV, 2, we additionally are meant to see that this arousing of desire will help to make Angelo's marriage to Mariana better than it would have been if he had lovelessly, politically married her as he intended to do before Frederick's death.

The knocking that we hear in IV, 2, seems to indicate the actual time that Angelo's heart is knowing Claudio's fault: first in the "momentary trick" and then in the aftermath. As soon as Angelo's heart does fully know, he invokes the authority that he thinks he alone holds. At the moment Angelo is both Claudio and the Duke. Isabella's speech may be said to have three parts: the medicine in authority that can "skin" vice, the knocking on the bosom in order to ask the heart, the tongue not "sounding." In IV, 2, though off stage, the absent Angelo is going through the parts or stages of Isabella's speech in reverse order: he doesn't sound a thought upon his tongue "in order to save" Claudio's life; he does know the heart; he invokes the medicine in authority in order to skin his vice by insisting that the death order be carried out before the designated time. Angelo's knowledge leads him to put himself before others, to act without mercy, to turn himself into a murderous tyrant.

If Angelo's aside in II, 2, is allowed to complete the last line of Isabella's speech and if a certain license in reading is permitted, the result is that they are together speaking "against my brother's life" in that Angelo's "sense" breeds with Isabella's "sense." In various ways the Duke as brother is involved, and the lines look back toward Isabella's brutal treatment of her brother when Claudio asks for mercy in prison. Apparently it is necessary for Isabella to discover her heart, to react with emotional violence, to be capable of bloody thoughts before she can move into understanding, before she can be the world's heart. After turning on a brother, Angelo and Isabella and the Duke are led to an understanding of self.

But Isabella's progress is of course strikingly different from Angelo's. Isabella is the misplaced heart; Angelo is the improper head. At the end Isabella will ask that the medicine in authority skin the vice of the top; she has asked her heart, and she will not sound a thought against Angelo's life. In fact she will ask that authority in the person of the Duke forgive an unbelievably evil deed: Isabella requests the medicine in authority that will skin vice; she wants vice skinned. In the seeming world of the beginning of the play Isabella's great act of Christian charity would be disastrous; Isabella is placed by the Duke in the position of realizing her magnificent potential. Earlier her actions would be against her "brother's" life, for a submission to Angelo's needs—to the needs of an uninstructed head—would destroy Claudio and the Duke.

A guilty Angelo would have to be punished. But of course Angelo is always safe because he is never really guilty. The Duke, with the increasing help of others, manages to pilot Angelo to safety. A true Duke must do all he can for each subject. In conjunction with the heart and the useful hand, the head avoids a general disaster. Finally, then, the parts of Isabella's speech, given above, are stages that the Duke passes quickly through in his own person: he has used medicine to skin the vice of the top; he has asked his heart; he does not sound a thought against his brother's life.

There is a reference to knocking in II, 2; there is actual knocking in IV, 2. Knocking on the stage in *Measure for Measure* should be loud and regular—the beating of a gigantic heart. Knocking is then a signal of urgency, a force that may be used to destroy but is necessary for creation. But to enable "the best and wholesomest spirits of the night" to envelop good, it is necessary to have a knight for good, to invoke a higher authority, to achieve a structure of human control. Angelo's coupling of passion with authority, of his using authority to serve his passion, demands that the Friar become again the Duke, that the Duke move into greater authority, that he refine passion and define authority, that he become a savior and a user of mercy. But the heart must be allowed to beat before man can be human. Isabella must enter and make herself felt: she must become the heart. Knocking then signifies the enormous change in Isabella and consequently in the world. Finally, knocking seems to represent the heart of collective man, the heart that must be allowed to beat and made to beat if man is to be alive and hopefully human.

VI

The Private and the Public View

As the world of *Measure for Measure* is re-created, each character finds a proper place and becomes a member of this world. The changed world is made to accommodate each individual. The main strategy used to illustrate the change in each character is the list—a series of terms or names or labels or roles. And it is our critical obligation to examine each particular set of items: first, in order to determine the relationship of one item to another; second, in order to understand the significance of the list to the total meaning of the play, the value of the list as a shorthand to meaning. For example, in III, 1, when Isabella tells Claudio that he might be freed if she will yield her virginity to Angelo, Claudio describes the horror of his Dantean end and then he begs her to let him live. Isabella's answer may be called a list of roles: "O you beast! / O faithless coward! O dishonest wretch! / Wilt thou be made a man out of my vice?"

Of course Isabella's invective expresses her heated, violent wrath, her instinctive revulsion. But the list of roles can also be seen as distinguishing the stages of Claudio's movement or development: when the Duke is initially in power, Claudio is a beast; when he is caught by the law, Claudio is a faithless coward; here in III, 1, Claudio is a dishonest wretch; in V, 1, he will be a man made new out of Isabella's "vice." The value of Isabella's list is, therefore, most fully perceived at the end of the play, and there the terms in her list of roles also apply in a different manner, for the items in the list seem finally objectified in and by specific characters: Barnardine is a beast; Lucio is a faithless coward; Angelo is a dishonest wretch; Claudio is a man made new. As the action moves toward the new Claudio, toward the reborn Claudio, the list is rendered in the play by actions and by actors.

In III, 2, the very next scene, another list of roles is presented. Lucio refers to the Duke as a "very superficial, ignorant, unweighing fellow," and, a few lines later, the Duke as Friar says that the Duke is "to the envious a scholar, a statesman, and a soldier." The Duke's nouns specifically balance Lucio's adjectives. Although Lucio's slander and malice are not accepted by us, we do see how and why the sophisticated, seeming public world of the beginning of the play could consider the Duke as being superficial, ignorant, and unweighing. Perhaps Lucio's adjectives are meant to qualify the Duke's nouns. For the Duke was, as he himself makes clear in I, 3, a person who "ever loved the life removed." He loved life when he was removed from it and it from him, and such a life, as the play vividly shows, is not human life at all. It may then be said that the Duke was a superficial scholar. His assumed role of Friar insists that he cease being a scholar and become an ignorant statesman, a person using craft. The Duke as Friar comes to realize that he must become an unweighing soldier for good.

The full list, which includes Lucio's term, serves to define the progress of the Duke. At first, as a young man, the Duke was a "very superficial, ignorant, unweighing fellow"; then he became a scholar; here in III, 2, he is a statesman; he will become a soldier. The great soldier was Frederick, Mariana's brother, and in IV, 1, the Duke takes the lost Frederick's place. The Duke's "To the envious" may indicate that the emerged ruler—the realized Duke, the Duke as soldier—is a qualification of the new Duke: "He who the sword of Heaven will bear / Should be as holy as severe."

Measure for Measure always seems to work from a public view and a private view, from what the world publicly seems and from what the world privately is. Here in III, 2, we are presented with Lucio and the Duke; we are to imagine Isabella and Angelo. If the comparable pair and their correlative action are added to Lucio and the Duke and their action here, the roles in the list are filled: Angelo is the "superficial, ignorant, unweighing fellow"; Lucio is the scholar; the Duke is the statesman; Isabella is the soldier.

Further, if the complicated configuration that is the play is to be perceived, we must see how the terms in Isabella's list, given above, may be said to apply to the Duke and to his movement: he is, at first, a beast, since he ignored ducal responsibility; he is, as Friar, a faithless coward, since he isn't really a

Friar at all; he is, as a user of craft, a dishonest wretch, since, for instance, he lets Isabella believe that her brother is dead; he is a man made out of vice, when Lucio uncowls him in V, 1. As in the first list of roles, where the items seem finally objectified in characters at the end, the list may enable us to see Barnardine as a "very superficial, ignorant, unweighing fellow"; Lucio as a scholar; Angelo as a statesman; Claudio, now a servant of good, as a soldier. Perhaps the main observation ought to be that as the other roles in various lists are filled, the Duke moves into being what he ideally is, into what the world demands that he become.

In IV, 3, Isabella and the Duke are on stage alone; he has just told her that Angelo has, after all, had Claudio killed. Isabella remarks:

> Unhappy Claudio! Wretched Isabel!
> Injurious world! Most damned Angelo!

The strange fact is that Isabella speaks of Claudio as if he is alive, and she speaks of herself as if she is someone else. The Isabel seen here is withdrawn into herself, detached from herself, as if there is another Isabel. Just as Lucio in III, 2, gives the Friar a true, public view of the Duke, so Isabella here gives the Friar a true, public view of the Duke. Claudio's unhappiness has led to Isabella's wretchedness, to the world's injuriousness, to Angelo's damnation. And the Duke, both as Friar and as father, is thoroughly implicated. Isabella's list in IV, 3, thrusts the Duke into a full recognition of what the world is and what the office of Duke demands. He must forcibly perceive that he must rule this vicious world. He prevents Angelo's damnation; he controls the injury that the world would do; he saves Isabella from wretchedness; he returns Claudio to happiness.

In V, 1, the long last scene of the play, at least four closely related lists of roles are easily discernible. The first list occurs at the beginning of the scene, when the Duke appears at the city gate in his own person and Isabella kneels and reports what she believes to be the savage truth about Angelo:

> That Angelo's forsworn, is it not strange?
> That Angelo's a murderer, is't not strange?
> That Angelo is an adulterous thief,

> An hypocrite, a virgin-violator,
> Is it not strange and strange?

When Angelo accepts the role of Duke, he becomes the instrument of justice, the wielder of power, the head, a figure of authority and responsibility. When he is seduced by Isabella, he allows a private desire to affect his public office, and his just punishment of Claudio is turned into an act of murder. In the garden house at night, he is an adulterous thief; after that, he is forced by his vanity into becoming a hypocrite. Just a moment before, in denying Isabella, he is verbally violating her, the virgin. A concatenation of strange, evil deeds is thus presented. But first, Angelo accepts the Duke's good commission. Angelo's forswearing goodness has brought him here to the city gate, where he will become part of a public spectacle before he is deliberately saved.

After Isabella is taken off, guarded, the Duke in his own person questions Mariana:

> *Duke.* What, are you married?
> *Mari.* No, my lord.
> *Duke.* Are you a maid?
> *Mari.* No, my lord.
> *Duke.* A widow, then?
> *Mari.* Neither, my lord.
> *Duke.* Why, you are nothing, then — neither
> maid, widow, nor wife?
> *Lucio.* My lord, she may be a punk, for many
> of them are neither maid, widow, nor
> wife.

The list is maid, widow, wife, punk. Isabella is the maid; Juliet is the widow; Mariana is the wife (in her next speech she will twice refer to Angelo as her husband); Kate Keepdown is the punk, a term that, significantly, Lucio adds to the list established by the Duke in the preceding line. At the end of the play, although Kate Keepdown is never seen, all four of the women are imaged as wives. The marriages are and will be the result of elaborate planning and enormous human involvement.

The order of maid, widow, wife seems strange until it is realized that each maid is left a kind of widow, is discarded, publicly cast aside, before she becomes or will become a wife. It is as if a true wife must first be a widow. The actuality of wives in the play is present only at the end. Now before the order in the list of roles is in fact given by the Duke, a prior list is given, a list that emerges out of the questions and answers between the Duke and Mariana. That list is "wife," maid, widow: the Duke first asks Mariana whether she is married. If Mariana isn't married, the other questions follow: her not being married makes the list possible. Isabella has made the "marriage" between Mariana and Angelo possible, and we know, as the Duke does, that Mariana's answers depend upon the "spirit" of Isabella.

All of the women in the play are just victims until Isabella asserts her will. Her refusal to be Angelo's punk saves her as maid and as eventual wife. Yet as a willful maid, Isabella was ready to let Claudio die, and this decision would have made Juliet a widow. By willingly obeying the Duke, Isabella makes it possible for the various roles to be appropriately filled: punk, maid, wife, widow. Moreover, Mariana's willingness to serve the Duke and be the wife keeps Isabella as the maid and insures that Mariana will be the necessary widow before she can be the true wife. If *strange* is the insistent word at the time of the first list in V, 1, *my lord* is the insistent locution in the second list.

Later in V, 1, Lucio says to the Duke, who is again back in his role as Friar, "Do you so, sir? And was the Duke a flesh-monger, a fool, and a coward, as you then reported him to be?" Of course the Duke says that Lucio must change places with the Friar because it was Lucio who called the Duke these names. We are meant to perceive, I think, how these terms do apply to the Duke. In giving his office to Angelo, the Duke was a coward of sorts. The Duke was a fool in a number of ways: he underestimated Angelo's capacity for evil; he didn't understand how much life could mean to a condemned man, like Claudio; he didn't understand how little life could mean to a hardened man, like Barnardine; he didn't realize what the world's opinion of himself as Duke was. Like Pompey, the Duke was a kind of fleshmonger in bringing a man and a woman, Angelo and Mariana, together.

The order of Lucio's list—fleshmonger, fool, coward—would seem significant. Perhaps we are meant to say that as soon as the Duke becomes a Friar, he is involving himself with human beings on their terms and that he is then a kind of fleshmonger. For the Duke to give up his power and to act in a powerless fashion as Friar is foolish, and such a Duke is a fool. Of course the witty intent is obvious: any human involvement is dangerous, foolish.[1] Since the Duke is now at the moment again disguised, he is again a kind of coward. Further, the order of Lucio's list readily applies to Lucio: he also goes from being a fleshmonger to being a fool to being a coward.

After Claudio has been unmuffled and restored to his original position, the Duke addresses Lucio:

> You, sirrah, that knew me for a fool, a coward,
> One all of luxury, an ass, a madman.

Part of our surprise is that the Duke would publicly speak as he does here; but, even though the Duke had earlier indicated that Lucio had said worse things about him, most of our surprise must be that the Duke changes what we have heard Lucio say. In other words, the Duke drops *fleshmonger* and adds *one all of luxury*, an *ass*, a *madman*. It is as if the Duke wants to make what Lucio said even worse than it really is. He seems strangely intent upon magnifying the slander. We may believe that the Duke's list of roles here proves that he has lost all vanity. By magnifying the slander, the Duke does underline Lucio's viciousness, and the result of this is to harden attitudes toward Lucio; perhaps the Duke intends to accentuate Lucio's malice so as to heighten the effect of his own grace when he finally reveals it and forgives Lucio. At any rate, the Duke freezes Lucio in misery and controls to a large extent the nature of Lucio's response.

The term *fleshmonger* may be dropped from the Duke's list because the Friar's role has been dropped: the Duke as Friar as fleshmonger is no more. But perhaps it is more meaningful to say that here at the end the Duke is acting as a marriage broker, a holy bawd, a fleshmonger. It is as if the Duke has dropped the first term in Lucio's list because the Duke is here acting as a fleshmonger; he has invested himself with the role. If we imagine the Duke's future to be the good fool, one who

---

[1] William Empson's *The Structure of Complex Words* (New York, 1951) is instructive, not only for his discussion of *sense* in *Measure for Measure* (pp. 270-284), but also for his other discussions, particularly that of *fool*.

can and does trust the world, we may suppose that Shakespeare is ironically suggesting that the other roles may also, or must also, follow. When the Duke goes back to the palace, he will then be a fool. If the Duke is acting like a fleshmonger at the moment, he may come to act like a fool, like a coward, and so on. It is as if Shakespeare is saying that the natural end of submitting one's self to the world is madness, for the world will in time become again a place of seeming.

But perhaps this is insisting on a reading that need not be insisted upon. In the famous advice to Claudio in prison, III, 1, the Duke declares that man is "death's fool" and that man is "like an ass." And we are not at a loss to find characters in the play to fill the roles in the Duke's list here, in V, 1. For example, Lucio in IV, 3, is clearly the ass, as his remark to Isabella quite explicitly proves: "O pretty Isabella, I am pale at mine heart to see thine eyes so red. Thou must be patient. I am fain to dine and sup with water and bran, I dare not for my head fill my belly, one fruitful meal would set me to 't." Lucio's answer to judicial pressure is to willingly consider himself an ass.

A human world is predicated upon a healthy body. And IV, 3, presents an actual head as well as Lucio's description of himself as an animal. The play remarkably demonstrates how dangerous and how desperate human life is, but that fact does not mean that the body can be ignored or that bodily needs can be perverted: man is an animal. The world needs order, but order isn't achieved through wanton denial. Pompey knows. If private needs are allowed to subvert public good, the world will soon become a place of license and injustice. But if private needs are allowed proper expression, they can work for the public good. Vanity is countered by love; slander is revealed by truth; self-centeredness is transmuted into regard for another human being. As sonnet 66 indicates, the only answer in a valueless world is love. Once the private and the public worlds are as one, the resultant world is human and valuable. Once those worlds are separate, life is unhuman and inhuman.

VII

Peace and Art

Generally speaking, the first three acts of a Shakespeare play establish the reality emerging out of the initial, seeming world of the play. By the end of Act III of *Hamlet* or *King Lear* the brutal possibilities of the beginning have been realized: Polonius has been killed; Gloucester has had his eyes put out. In the last two acts of a Shakespeare play something is added to reality, to that which life existentially is: value and meaning are added; human feeling is made effective. In *King Lear* the word used to signify this new, added element is *Heaven*. Only after Lear has turned from being a king into being a poor, bare man does Cordelia return to Britain. After a significant loss, a substantial gain is realized. After murdering Polonius, Hamlet leaves Denmark, and then he comes back, naked. In a Shakespeare play reality is established. Then Heaven or the soul or the spirit comes back to the world, makes itself felt in the world, re-invests the real world. In *Measure for Measure* the world becomes real, and then Isabella becomes the spirit of goodness or of spiritual health.

The world of a Shakespeare tragedy rushes to its apparently inevitable end; the world of a Shakespeare comedy is simply granted peace. The world of *Twelfth Night* or *As You Like It* can be destroyed; it is saved by a miracle. In other words, the end of a Shakespeare comedy comes to depend upon Shakespeare's art. Reality; then Heaven; then art. Since, typically, a Shakespeare comedy comes close to disaster in the second half of its action, art is needed in order to effect peace. It is as if Shakespeare insists that *his* art makes the concord possible. In Shakespearean comedy, we, the audience, are meant to be aware that without the hand of the artist, the play would not end happily. The concord at the end is established by stages and in stages, and as we watch the action, we can perceive the fortunate events that determine happiness. In the real world the happiness would never be achieved. And as the play world becomes real, we are intended to understand that the happiness would never be achieved without the intervention of the artist, without some outside force. That is to say, the world of a Shakespeare comedy is made peaceful and well at the end and by the end.

In I, 4, before Lucio enters the nunnery of Saint Clare, his offstage voice is heard: "Ho! Peace be in this place!" In IV, 3, before Isabella enters the prison, her offstage voice is heard: "Peace ho, be here!" The similarity of the two situations, of the two offstage lines, and of the two entrances indicates an elaborate relationship. Lucio comes from Claudio; Isabella comes from Angelo. Lucio needs the services of Isabella; Isabella needs the services of the Duke. Lucio in effect makes a demand that Isabella give up being a religious sister, a nun, in order to enter the secular world; Isabella in effect makes a demand that the Duke stop being a brother, the Friar, in order to become something more, the father, the ruler. The action may be seen as moving from the situation in I, 4, to the situation in IV, 3, from one offstage line to another offstage line. A number of characters is involved.

Ho would seem to have been pronounced like *Oh,* and in any case the sounds are similar. If *Ho* is considered to be *O* and if *O* is seen as Shakespeare's sign of concord, his symbol for order, for inclusiveness, for the world,[1] Lucio may be said to be addressing O, and Lucio is in a sense then expressing the hope or the wish that peace be in the cloister. Isabella and Francisca have just been talking about privileges and restraints, about private peace, and then Lucio's voice is heard: "Ho! Peace be in this place!" In the cloister peace depends upon rules and restrictions, upon inhibitions and impositions. The initial need for peace is a need for something not to be found in the temporal world. In a sense then, O, the world, makes peace in the convent both possible and necessary. Peace in a prison will enable peace to be found in the world.

Peace in a convent is to be expected; peace in a prison is to be expected too, but it is of a different kind. In a convent peace is the expression of inner desire; in a prison peace is

---

[1] In the Prologue to *Henry V* the wooden O is explicitly the Globe Theater, as if to insist on the identification of the O with the globe, the world. Obviously the trope employed is the Shakespearean commonplace that all the world is a stage.

the result of outer pressure. Symbolically, the initial, disordered world of *Measure for Measure* must enter the prison before it can be released to normal living. In IV, 3, the Duke as Friar and the Provost speak, and then Isabella's voice is heard: "Peace ho, be here!" In a sense Isabella is addressing O and is asking that peace be in the prison. She doesn't know that her Friar is her Duke and that at the moment he must be more concerned with Vienna, his world, than he is with her or with Claudio. The Duke must become the proper father. True worldly peace demands that the Duke reassume his proper authority. But it is not yet time for him to reveal himself; it is not yet time for him to be revealed.

The Provost exits *carrying a head,* and then Isabella's voice is heard: "Peace ho, be here!" The head is Razozine's; it will take the place of Barnardine's head; it is then Claudio's head, so Angelo will think. If Isabella were to enter without first speaking, she would perhaps see the head and perhaps see that it is not her brother's head. For peace to remain in the prison, it is necessary that an awkward meeting between the Provost and Isabella be avoided. Thus the Duke's successful plot seems to depend here upon the Provost's rapid exit; the Duke as Friar is almost caught by the returning Isabella. The movement on stage is a heightened piece of tricky, ironic business.

Consummate peace here depends upon Isabella's continued ignorance. In this scene the Provost and the Duke are lucky to hear Isabella before she enters. Then the Duke deliberately lies to Isabella: Angelo, she is told, has had Claudio killed. Although Isabella becomes furious at Angelo, the Duke as Friar is able to contain her anger. The Duke's wit and Isabella's willingness to be directed by this Friar determine peace. But the Duke's good intentions are always extended by ironic developments. The Duke tells Claudio that life is meaningless, and then Barnardine, a living illustration of the Duke's thesis, is presented. After Isabella agrees to serve the Duke as Friar, Barnardine refuses to serve the Duke as Friar. Here, in IV, 3, the Duke simply needs Barnardine to act as he apparently should be willing to act: all that careless Barnardine has to agree to do is to willingly give up his meaningless life, just a few hours before the appointed time. But Barnardine refuses to die this day, and the Duke as Friar is surprised and caught. In multiple ways they are all saved by Ragozine's death, by his head, by the way that that head is employed.

The Duke and the Provost are using the death of Ragozine as the means of craft. The head is carried off, and the tongue of the heart is heard. Hopefully, a peaceful O, a meaningful O, will result. As Isabella comes on stage, she remarks, "Ho, by your leave!" O can be achieved only by and through the Duke. He will at once lie to Isabella. The Duke must *leave* his role as Friar in order for the O to be achieved. Peace must come before the O. O insures peace. But both peace and O depend upon craft and are thus morally tenuous. Still, peace and O are achieved. And these three short lines can be seen, I think, as one kind of paradigm of *Measure for Measure:* "Ho! Peace be in this place!" "Peace ho, be here!" "Ho, by your leave!"

Barnardine, that gravel heart, refuses to die and let his head become a substitute for Claudio's. The Provost announces that a prisoner has died that morning of a cruel fever, and the Duke as Friar remarks:

> Oh, 'tis an accident that Heaven provides!
> Dispatch it presently, the hour draws on
> Prefixed by Angelo.

The reference of *'tis* is to the death of Ragozine, a notorious pirate "of Claudio's years, his beard and head / Just of his color."[2] It seems unsuitable arrogance for the Friar to speak of a man's death as something provided by Heaven. Heaven has come into the world, and it provides this. But the Duke of course means that Ragozine is exactly the person that the Duke as Friar and the Duke as Duke needs, the person that the occasion demands.

"Dispatch it presently." The antecedent of *it* is Ragozine, the head of Ragozine. The head will be sent to Angelo as a sign that the execution has occurred. But *'tis* in the previous line suggests that the antecedent of *it* may also be the *accident* or *O*. The fortunate, timely death of this pirate will make possible an O, peace, concord. O is the product of an accident.

---

[2] If Ragozine is like Claudio, then he is like Barnardine and like Angelo. Biblically, Ragozine and his lost head would seem to represent John the Baptist. In the play Ragozine is the scapegoat for Claudio, Barnardine, Angelo.

Further, the word *Heaven* may signify that *Dis* is to be seen in the word *Dispatch*. If so, the implication is that *Dis,* the underworld (metaphorically the prison), will patch or mend *it,* the O. The fact that the pirate has gone to Hell enables Claudio and Barnardine to remain on earth. In addition, then, *it* may refer to Heaven, as if Hell is being used to patch Heaven. The final concord will result from the use of the underworld, the prison, that which is unseen. The words may be read in a slightly different way: "Oh, 'tis an accident that Heaven provides Dis. Patch it presently." *It* may now refer to Heaven or to Dis or to the accident that it is Heaven that provides Dis.

Since Dis is also Pluto, the Duke may perhaps he seen as the god of the underworld, who will patch or mend. As the ruler in the prison, with the Provost at his service, the Duke is controlling Angelo, the substitute Duke, and he is thus employing the power of a god, a prison god, an imprisoned god. As the speaker of the lines under consideration, the Duke may be seen as addressing the Provost as Dis. This would make the Duke a greater god. Then too it may be possible to see Angelo as Dis or Pluto: he has become a god who operates in the dark, out of sight. When Isabella enters, she may be seen as a kind of Proserpina, the present "wife" of Angelo, the future wife of the Duke. If the reference here in Act IV is to the power of Hell, the reference in the last scene of the play is to the Duke as holding the power of Heaven. After the Friar is revealed to be the Duke, outside the prison, at the city gate, Angelo comments, "When I perceive your Grace, like power divine, / Hath looked upon my passes."

Before the pun on *Dispatch* is dismissed as being only fancied, consideration should be given to the nature of the concord at the end of the play. If, for example, there were no Ragozine (if he had not been a pirate, if he had not been caught, if he had not fortunately died), if his head were not very similar to Claudio's, the Duke as Friar would be drawn into doing something here that would lesson the force and value of the end. The least he would have to do would be to reveal more of himself than he would like. The action would never reach Act V. Furthermore, the Duke's power as Friar in Act IV is explicitly given its limitations: he is defeated by Barnardine's stubbornness; he is brought to lie to Isabella.

The realization that the Friar is stultified by the behavior and attitudes of others is the central lesson learned by the Duke as Friar. In fact, his use of craft against vice has lured him into behaving more like a god than like a disguised Duke. And the Duke is only a man, different from a friar, less than a god. The world needs a father's control, and the Duke comes to perceive the necessity of his becoming in truth the father so that peace can be insured. Since he has been made to go beyond the role of brother, he must become a proper father, one who publicly is what he seems.

When Isabella kneels beside Mariana before the Duke at last, she is pleading for her friend, for a family, for life. To her Claudio is dead; she believes that nothing can remedy that loss. But if Angelo is destroyed, then Mariana will be bereft of what she desires; she will be as she had been when forsaken by Angelo. Moreover, Isabella owes Mariana a debt for the help given in the garden house. If Isabella cares, she must do as her friend requests. If Isabella cares about human kind, she must help every other human being. To Isabella, the choice must now be simple. Either Isabella demands death, or she yields to life. Either she demands justice, or she pleads for mercy. Either she insists upon Hell, or she opts for Heaven.

Still, Dis, the underworld, the prison, determines concord. Heaven or the spirit or Isabella has entered the world, but her presence isn't enough. In the real world the truth (Angelo's duplicity; the Duke's virtue) would be divulged, divulged for primitive, foolish, accidental reasons, and, once divulged, the truth would be no longer true. Shakespeare controls truth, controls the action. In other words, Shakespeare controls Dis, controls by his art that which is in the real world uncontrollable. Shakespeare emphasizes the brutal, thoughtless conditions that would really undermine happiness. In this way, Shakespeare wants us to understand all that is needed in order for the best human end to be achieved and attained. We, the audience, are meant to perceive that the fine end of *Measure for Measure* depends upon the body, on the patching that Dis, Pluto, the underworld, the prison, can do and is made to do in the play.

"The hour draws on / Prefixed by Angelo." Angelo has set the time for the delivered head, and the Duke and the Provost must act in accordance with Angelo's prescription. But at the time of the play's first performance *hour* was pronounced like *whore*,[3] and the reference then seems to be to Isabella, who Angelo thinks has become a whore. Isabella will soon arrive at the prison, as if to insist that she comes as *the* whore: since her last appearance on stage, the assignation in the garden house has taken place. Angelo thinks that he has turned Isabella into a whore, someone he can discard. The named but absent whore in the play is Kate Keepdown, Lucio's forgotten prostitute. In that Mariana has given herself to Angelo, she has become a kind of whore. Mariana was discarded; then she becomes a whore. First, Angelo is fixed in place, "prefixed," caught and doomed; then the whore is needed in the world, by the world. After Pluto or Hell has patched O, the whore will draw the concord on. Isabella and Mariana and Juliet and Kate Keepdown will draw the world to its fortunate end.

When Mariana and Isabella kneel before the Duke at last, they are behaving in a manner finer and better than the Duke could have hoped or that we at the beginning could have imagined. The excellent behavior of Isabella is not demeaned by our awareness of all that the occasion depends upon. Though, since she can bend, she is metaphorically a whore, Isabella is wonderful. It is, I think, a major portion of Shakespeare's intent that, as the action moves to the city gate, we are made increasingly aware of the outside world. The imagined, created world of *Measure for Measure* is deliberately constructed: the artistic, safe world at the end is created out of the real, brutal world. Thus we are meant to be increasingly aware of the invisible Shakespeare at work, the artist at work, the Shakespeare behind the Duke. First, the Duke; then, Shakespeare. Every major character is brought to the edge of destruction, and then that character is saved by the Duke and by Shakespeare. Man is made human by virtue of difficult choices. Consequently, we are presented with a true, brutal view of the way life actually is; then we are made to understand what meaningful life depends upon, what peace depends upon. Art determines the answer; and the answer is largely art.

---

[3] There is a widespread awareness of this pun in Shakespeare. See Alfred Harbage, *William Shakespeare: A Reader's Guide* (New York, 1963), p. 11.

VIII

"Stage Me to Their Eyes"

Although critics have complained about the end of *Measure for Measure*,[1] the long last scene is a deliberate spectacle, not something careless or inartistic: all of its risks as drama are consciously run. It has no soliloquies and no asides; its action is all public, a gathering together of all of the major characters, as if the intent is to bring to a head all that has been so far established. In the first scene of the play the Duke says that he does not like to be staged to their eyes, yet at the end he insists upon doing that which he professedly despises. His willingness to stage himself at the end demonstrates his loss of vanity, his readiness to accept full public responsibility, his desire for a disclosure of the past. In the last act the Duke is the conscious stage director and a chief actor.

The long scene that is the last act begins with the Duke entering in his own person and addressing Angelo and Escalus, who then together answer: "Happy returns to your royal Grace!" After taking Angelo's hand, the Duke speaks:

> Come, Escalus,
> You must walk by us on our other hand.
> And good supporters are you.

The Duke on stage is flanked by Angelo and Escalus, the Duke and his two seconds on stage. The interesting, visual fact is that this beginning is exactly comparable to the beginning of I, 1. The Duke's public return is like the beginning of his private retreat.

The Duke first appears in the scene in his own person; then he leaves and comes back dressed as the Friar; then the Friar is revealed to be the Duke in disguise. The Duke's changes in

---

[1] Theodore Spencer, for example, makes this comment: "The last act of *Measure for Measure* . . . is a kind of desperate attempt to give a 'happy' ending to what is essentially a tragic theme; the reconciliations, which have no right to be reconciliations, are, as it were, plastered over the basically tragic material." (Theodore Spencer, *Shakespeare and the Nature of Man* (New York, 1942), p. 184.)

costume and his exits and entrances in V, 1, may then be said to signify the symbolic progress of the Duke in the total play. He begins as the Duke; he is the Friar; he is the Duke as Friar; he is the Friar as Duke. During the last one hundred and forty lines of the play he is the public Duke, though still dressed as the Friar: he is a visible brother-father. In other words, the scene presents a shorthand or condensed version of the Duke's progress, a public statement of what the Duke's private progress has been: that is to say, V, 1, is the entire dramatic action in another key.

The end is new, *after* the final scene recapitulates the entire play. It is as if Shakespeare first wants to rehearse the movement of the Duke from being what he seemed to be into being what he is. When the Duke enters in V, 1, he is publicly now what the usual world of Vienna has all the time thought. His appearance now is what his public appearance was. Of course we, the audience, know that the Duke has been active as a brother in the city. The world of Vienna is surprised by the various disclosures; we are not surprised because we have seen the disclosures as they were being dramatically presented *to us*. In part then the last scene is a dramatic, metaphoric, symbolic summation, one that cogently restates and reinforces the development of the total play.

In other words, Lucio's unmasking of the Duke in V, 1, is comparable to the metaphoric unmasking given by Lucio in III, 2. The verbal revealing takes place in the middle of the play; the visual revealing takes place in the middle of the final scene. Only the Duke is on stage to hear about himself in Act III; almost everyone is on stage to see the Duke realized in Act V. At the beginning of the play the Duke and the Duke as Friar are quite distinct, to the Duke himself and to us, the audience. But in III, 2, the Duke as Friar is presented with Lucio's "public" Duke, a different person, an unrealized aspect that the Duke must control or subsume. In wearing the Friar's costume at the end, the Duke is patently a father and a brother.[2]

---

[2] At the beginning of III, 2, Elbow addresses the disguised Duke as "good Father Friar," to which the Duke replies, "And you, good Brother Father." Elbow's foolish mistaking foreshadows the visual truth in V, 1. In IV, 3, when the Duke tells the Provost to dispatch Ragozine's head, the Provost replies: "This shall be done, good Father, presently."

Part of the reason for the presence of Friar Peter in the last three scenes of the play is to emphasize the difference at the end between two adequately filled roles: Friar Peter visually picks up and fulfills the role that the new Duke surrenders. When in IV, 5, the Duke appears on stage in his own person again, Friar Peter is with him. The Friar in I, 4, is Thomas, the twin; the Friar at the end is Peter, the rock. The appearance of Friar Peter serves to prove that the Duke is no longer a Friar. There is a "real" Friar, and, as a substitute for the Duke as Friar, he enters the service of the emerging Duke. In his next-to-last speech in the play, Friar Peter says that he has come from Friar Lodowick, the Duke as Friar, "To speak, as from his mouth." When the Duke leaves and returns as Lodowick, Friar Peter subsides into being a good brother. Presumably Friar Peter will continue the work started by his master.

When Isabella kneels to the Duke at the beginning of V, 1, she is kneeling as she had done to Angelo in Act II. Thus her actions in V, 1, until the end correspond to her actions in the first four acts. The main difference now, in the first part of Act V, is that the real Duke, now corrected and instructed, is back in his enriched place, holding his rightful office. All of the actions that were so dangerous before are only the means of the Duke's public exposure. Since the Duke and we have heard the private exposure in III, 2, we desire it to happen again now: it must happen now so that the play world may see. The hidden, tentative, vain actions are repeated so that these actions may work for good. The Duke is in control of the action, until he is surprised by Isabella's wonderful behavior at the end. The Duke surprisingly provides Isabella with the occasion for showing her magnificence. The Duke surprises us by announcing his intention of becoming Isabella's husband.

Chairs are used as props in Act V. After Isabella is carried off, guarded, the Duke orders, "Give us some seats." It seems clear that two chairs are brought on stage; the Duke and Angelo are seated during the time that Mariana presents the case against her "husband." Later the Duke says, "You, Lord Escalus, / Sit with my cousin." Escalus takes the vacant chair, and the Duke goes off stage. After the Duke comes back as the Friar and is uncowled by Lucio, Escalus rises from his chair. The Duke tells Escalus to sit down and then he turns to Angelo and says, "We'll borrow place of him." And while Escalus and the Duke sit, Angelo leaves with Mariana and Friar Peter. Later Mariana and Isabella kneel before the seated Duke and Escalus.

One of the two chairs is the Elizabethan "chair of state."[3] First, the Duke has Angelo sit in it, and then the Duke rightfully takes it. Before the end of the play the Duke is in the chair of state and Escalus is sitting at his side. When the Duke tells the kneeling Mariana to stand up, she must rise, and we assume that Isabella also rises. After Claudio is unmuffled, the Duke tells Isabella to give him her hand. It would seem likely that the Duke would stand now, while holding Isabella's hand. At any rate it seems that everyone would be on his feet at the end. Although *Exeunt Omnes* is not in the Folio as a stage direction, the actors would probably leave the stage in pairs.[4] But, however the actors leave the stage, the two chairs probably remain, perhaps in order to mock us with their presence and by their emptiness. In this way the action is delivered to us, the audience. As we leave the theatre, the moral dialectic should fill our minds. The Duke as stage manager and as actor gives way to Shakespeare as artist, and we are left with the burden of living.

Measure for Measure ends with this couplet:
 So bring us to our palace, where we'll show
 What's yet behind, that's meet you all should know.

Thus the last lines indicate that part of the past is still hidden and that it will be divulged: all will be divulged that is meet or proper for the others to know at the palace. Moreover, the Duke is now alert to the danger of revealing all: as the head, he must decide what can or should be revealed. *Meet* is then of course also *mete,* to judge; and the Duke as the best exponent of justice, as the manager of the revealed world, establishes the relevance of the pun. It is as if the informed Duke has already judged and will judge the past in order to decide what the others should know of it. If *we*

---

[3] See W. Moelwyn Merchant, *Shakespeare and the Artist* (London, 1959), pp. 229-232.
[4] See the footnote in Lever, p. 149.

refers to both Isabella and himself as Duke, *he* must still decide. The Duke comes to realize that he should not or cannot reveal all of the past.

Even now, with the Duke's last couplet, while the Duke is pluming himself up over his superior knowledge, we are perhaps meant to see the probability of future disaster. The Duke has just said to Angelo about Mariana: "I have confessed her, and I know her virtue." It is inappropriate for a "seeming" Friar to confess a maid. And perhaps a vulnerable Mariana still cannot be trusted. Right after the song, which renders the play's answer to the problem of human life, Mariana's first words are these: "Break off thy song, and haste thee quick away." Clearly, Mariana and Angelo, though saved as man and wife, will never be completely safe; but so long as the Duke and Isabella keep control, Vienna will be as secure as a human community can ever be.

The palace is the place of authority, where the Duke will reassume his proper responsibility. A holy and severe Duke cannot *seem* to be other than this Duke seems here and presumably seemed at the palace before the action of the play. But, fortunately, the Duke will marry Isabella; the caught characters have been shown some truth; instruction and correction have taken place. But, still, nothing is enough; the history of the world makes clear that nothing is enough. But, again, the movement within a Shakespeare play is back to the metaphoric garden, to a symbolic spring. The past will not be fully divulged; the future is unknown. And outside the play, life must still be lived by us; time must still be served by us. Spring is the symbolic answer in the play; and though spring is the place to which the action is brought, the play is not life.

Shakespearean comedy ends with concord, but we are meant to see further, to see that the concord is only a stasis, a momentarily safe thing. The end of a Shakespeare play is just the last, the final statement of the play, the conclusion reached by the dialectic of the action: it is the statement that culminates the action or caps the various parts. The total poetic statement is what causality in Shakespeare means, what plot in Shakespeare is. After the world has been corrected and instructed, made new, then the process has to begin again.

Anything else is unhuman and inhuman. Just as the characters leave to go to the palace, so the play gives way to life. Just as we leave the theatre, life must leave the garden. Life has to be resubmitted to time, to the world. We come to see that finally *Measure for Measure,* like every other Shakespeare play, is a symbolic statement of the nature of man. It is other things, and it is prior things, but, essentially, ultimately, it is a rendered artistic expression of what being human means.

A Selected Bibliography

Battenhouse, Roy. *"Measure for Measure* and the Christian Doctrine of the Atonement," *Publication of the Modern Language Association,* LXI (1946), 1029-1059.

Bradbrook, M. C. "Authority, Truth, and Justice in *Measure for Measure,*" *Review of English Studies,* XVII (1942), 385-399.

Campbell, Oscar J. *Shakespeare's Satire.* Oxford, 1948.

Caputi, Anthony. "Scenic Design in *Measure for Measure,*" *Journal of English and Germanic Philology,* XL (1961), 423-434.

Chambers, E. K. *Shakespeare: A Survey.* London, 1925.

Chambers, R. W. *Man's Unconquerable Mind.* London, 1939.

Charlton, H. B. *Shakespearean Comedy.* London, 1938.

Coghill, Nevill. "Comic Form in *Measure for Measure,*" *Shakespeare Survey,* 8 (1955), 14-26.

Dunkel, Wilbur. "Law and Equity in *Measure for Measure,*" *Shakespeare Quarterly,* XIII (1962), 276-285.

Empson, William. *Seven Types of Ambiguity.* London, 1949.

———. *The Structure of Complex Words.* New York, 1951.

Evans, Bertrand. *Shakespeare's Comedies.* Oxford, 1960.

Fergusson, Francis. *The Human Image in Dramatic Literature.* New York, 1957.

Goddard, Harold C. *The Meaning of Shakespeare.* (2 vols.) Chicago, 1962.

Harbage, Alfred. *William Shakespeare: A Reader's Guide.* New York, 1963.

Harrison, George B. (ed.). *Shakespeare: the Complete Works.* New York, 1952.

Harrison, John L. "The Convention of 'Heart' and 'Tongue' and the Meaning of *Measure for Measure,*" *Shakespeare Quarterly,* V (1954), 1-10.

Knight, G. Wilson. *The Wheel of Fire.* London, 1949.

Knights, L. C. "The Ambiguity of *Measure for Measure,*" *Scrutiny,* X (1942), 222-233.

Lascelles, Mary. *Shakespeare's "Measure for Measure."* London, 1953.

Lawrence, W. W. *Shakespeare's Problem Comedies.* New York, 1960.

Leavis, F. R. *The Common Pursuit.* London, 1952.

Leech, Clifford. "The Meaning of *Measure for Measure,*" *Shakespeare Survey,* 3 (1950), 66-73.

Lever, J. W. (ed.). *The Arden Shakespeare: "Measure for Measure."* London, 1965.

Mackay, Eileen. *"Measure for Measure,"* Shakespeare Quarterly, XIV (1963), 109-113.

Marsh, D. R. C. "The Mood of *Measure for Measure,"* Shakespeare Quarterly, XIV (1963), 31-38.

Merchant, W. Moelwyn. *Shakespeare and the Artist.* London, 1959.

Millet, Stanton. "The Structure of *Measure for Measure,"* Boston University Studies in English, II (1956), 207-217.

Nagarajan, S. (ed.). *The Signet Classic Shakespeare:* "Measure for Measure." New York, 1964.

Nathan, Norman. "The Marriage of Duke Vincentio and Isabella," Shakespeare Quarterly, VII (1956), 43-45.

Ornstein, Robert. *The Moral Vision of Jacobean Tragedy.* Madison, 1960.

Pope, Elizabeth Marie. "The Renaissance Background of *Measure for Measure,"* Shakespeare Survey, 2 (1949), 66-82.

Quiller-Couch, Sir Arthur and J. Dover Wilson. (eds.). *New Cambridge Edition of Shakespeare.* Cambridge, 1922.

Righter, Anne. *Shakespeare and the Idea of the Play.* London, 1962.

Roscelli, William John. "Isabella, Sin and Civil Law," *University of Kansas City Review,* XXVIII (1962), 215-227.

Schanzer, Ernest. *The Problem Plays of Shakespeare.* London, 1963.

Siegel, P. M. *"Measure for Measure:* the Significance of the Title," Shakespeare Quarterly, IV (1953), 375-384.

Sisson, Charles J. *The Mythical Sorrows of Shakespeare.* London, 1934.

Smith, Robert M. "Interpretations of *Measure for Measure,"* Shakespeare Quarterly, I (1950), 208-218.

Smith, Warren D. "More Light on *Measure for Measure,"* Modern Language Quarterly, XXIII (1962), 301-322.

Spencer, Theodore. *Shakespeare and the Nature of Man.* New York, 1942.

Stauffer, Donald A. *Shakespeare's World of Images.* New York, 1949.

Stevenson, David L. "Design and Structure in *Measure for Measure:* A New Appraisal," *Journal of English Literary History,* XXIII (1956), 256-278.

Tillyard, E. M. W. *Shakespeare's Last Plays.* London, 1951.

———. *Shakespeare's Problem Plays.* London, 1950.

Traversi, D. A. *An Approach to Shakespeare. New York,* 1956.

Wilson, H. S. "Action and Symbol in *Measure for Measure,"* Shakespeare Quarterly, IV (1953), 375-384.